On the author

Fred Traguth is a singular phenomenon on the German and international dance scene. He is passionately devoted to jazz and modern dance both of which he has helped to popularize both in and outside of Germany.

Traguth was born in Stuttgart and began attending the Folkwang Schule in Essen in 1957. His teachers there included Kurt Jooss. From there he went to New York where he attended George Balanchine's School of American Ballet, the International School of Dance and the Martha Graham School.

After working as a solo dancer in Ulm he taught choreography from 1961 to 1963 at the Schola Cantorum in Paris, and then in Cologne. In 1965 he was appointed Professor of Modern Dance at the University of Bahia (Brasil) where he founded the "Grupo de Dança Contemporanea".

Besides guest lectureships in Brno, Prague, Cannes, Munich and cities in Austria and Switzerland he has held countless introductory lectures on jazz and modern dance that he accompanies with demonstrations. His name has figured on the program at the International Youth Music Festival in Bayreuth, at the Ruhr Music Festival in Recklinghausen and at the International Seminar for Rhythmic Dance in Remscheid. In Bonn he created a Seminar for Jazz and Modern Dance. In 1973 he began there with what is one of his most important activities, the "International Dance Workshop in Bonn" which is attended by both amateurs and professionals (over 400 thus far). Besides jazz and modern dance, mimic creativity, primitive and folk dance are taught. There is an excellent choreographic workshop taught by Traguth himself, a music workshop as well as a class in kinesiotherapy.

Traguth regularly spends several months abroad for study purposes. In 1976, for example, he was in Africa (Accra, Ghana) and New York where he studied jazz dance with David Harris and Frank Wagner, modern dance with Murray Louis and kinesiology with Raoul Gelabert.

Fred Traguth has produced important choreographies: "Protest" 1959, "Frequenzen I" 1965, "Brasilianische Impressionen" 1966, "Frequenzen II", "Collage I" both 1967, "Les Structures Sonores" 1968, "Collage II", "running" both 1974, "Mister Saxophone" 1975, "in silence" 1976 and since 1969 a ballet workshop that has put out various productions.

Among Fred Traguth's publications are: "Die Einheit des Modernen Tanzes" (1966), "Jazz Dance" (1970), "Choreographie heute" (1971), "Die Zukunft des Ballets beginnt immer wieder neu" (1974).

Helmut Scheier

On this book

The present volume is intended to help alleviate an acute
lack of professional and practical information on the subject of modern jazz dance. It is meant to be an aid to the interested amateur, as well as the professional, who is in se-
arch of new forms. It offers him an introduction and a
chance of establishing himself in this complex discipline.
The author has attempted to create a clear practical approach with a minimum of theoretical ballast.
No book on this subject has ever before been published
that has tried to overcome the dividing line that still exists
between the professional and amateur camps. I hope that
everyone interested will benefit from the suggested exercises and be inspired to further initiative.
Besides providing training in developing dance techniques many of these exercises also have considerable therapeutic value.
Dance and dance technique seen from an educational point of view represent an approach which involves the individual in his totality. This point needs to be emphasized.
This book is addressed to a much broader public than just
professional circles. I want it to penetrate the grey zones of
public opinion and thoroughly correct the false notions the
general public has of what jazz dance is all about. It is already an indisputable fact that dance in its contemporary
role has not only broken down social barriers but has also
helped to form new life styles.

FRED TRAGUTH
Author/Editor

To DANCE, its future,
creative powers
and human message

**FRED TRAGUTH
OTTO HANDTKE**

MODERN JAZZ
DANCE

A SPECTRUM BOOK

Prentice-Hall, Inc., Englewood Cliffs, N.J. 07632

Library of Congress Cataloging in Publication Data

Traguth, Fred.
  Modern jazz dance.

  Reprint. Originally published: New York : Dance
Motion Press, ©1978.
  "A Spectrum book."
  Bibliography: p.
  1. Jazz dance.   I. Title.
[GV1753.T7 1983]   793.3   82-25066
ISBN 0-13-595009-0
ISBN 0-13-594994-7 (pbk.)

10   9   8   7   6   5   4   3   2   1

ISBN 0-13-595009-0

ISBN 0-13-594994-7 {PBK.}

THE DANCERS
Ulrike Fassl/Germany
Francis Carty/England
James Saunders/USA

Cover design and layout by Otto Handtke

Prentice-Hall International, Inc., *London*
Prentice-Hall of Australia Pty. Limited, *Sydney*
Prentice-Hall Canada Inc., *Toronto*
Prentice-Hall of India Private Limited, *New Delhi*
Prentice-Hall of Japan, Inc., *Tokyo*
Prentice-Hall of Southeast Asia Pte. Ltd., *Singapore*
Whitehall Books Limited, Wellington, *New Zealand*
Editora Prentice-Hall do Brasil Ltda., *Rio de Janeiro*

Foreword

Basically, it is the same with jazz dance as it with modern dance – it is precisely what everyone understands it to be. In contrast to the classical and academic dance of ballet, neither of them recognize any kind of restrictions, either in their definition or their rules of performance. Just as in modern dance where we have the distinct systems of Martha Graham and Doris Humphrey (just to name two from a large number of individual styles), a quick look at the classes of, say, Matt Mattox, Luigi, Walter Nicks, Donald McKayle, or Gus Giordano is enough to make anyone realize that jazz dance is not always interpreted the same way. Even though German experts continue to try to rescue the concept of isolation movements as a common denominator of all the different personal variants of jazz dance, this, too, is nothing more than an individualistic hobby. Neither the Encyclopedia Britannica (in its entry "Jazz Dance") nor Marshall and Jean Sterns (in their standard work *Jazz Dance* use this concept. The importance of isolation movements for one person is the indispensable tie to jazz music for another, while a third may consider swing the decisive characteristic of all jazz dance.

I am afraid that there will be no one binding definition of jazz dance as long as there is no agreement on a general definition of jazz itself. "It can be heard, felt and seen but it is very difficult to define": What Marshall and Jean Stearns say of swing is also true of jazz and jazz dance.

It would probably be easiest to reach agreement on the statement that jazz dance is a mixture of African and European dance that, in this form, could only have originated on American soil, and that it has developed more or less parallel to jazz music. It is the proportions of this mixture that determine its various manifest forms, and it is apparently here that everyone who feels the need to express himself on the phenomenon jazz dance draws his dividing lines.

For some, pure jazz dance is only conceivable as individual self-realization of the dancer on the dance floor, while for others it is considered an art product meant to be seen on stage. There are a great many different performers and teachers and, consequently, a great many different techniques and styles.

Most confusing of all is talking with choreographers about their ideas on jazz dance and jazz ballet. Alvin Ailey's *Revelations* based on gospel songs, spirituals and blues, are for some not jazz ballet precisely because of their musical basis (similarly McKayles' *Rainbow Round My Shoulder*), but a work like Jerome Robbin's *New York Export: Op. Jazz* is even less so. In his all too numerous ballets based on music by Duke Ellington, Ailey is accused of selling out jazz ballet to show business.

Is it possible that legitimate jazz dance doesn't even exist – that it is merely a figment of our individual imagination? The fact that individuality plays such an important, if not, indeed, the most important role in it, seems to me to be at the center of its vitality in the face of which all theoretical definition dissolves away — altogether in keeping with the individual character of jazz music. This is doubtless where its immense attraction lies for those people who feel frustrated by the strict discipline, i. e. by the social or artistic constraints of other dance forms, who see in it a more spontaneous and elementary means of self-realization and experience as a dancer, perhaps the only one left in our totally organized world.

I suspect that things will go well for jazz dance, that it will retain its originality and vitality as long as the theoreticians, systemizers and historians are not able to pin it down. And it would appear that, for the moment at least, they nowhere near doing this.

Horst Koegler

Contents

Modern Jazz Dance –
Only a Misunderstanding?

The present book represents an attempt to make a constructive contribution to the subject of jazz dance in the Federal Republic and possibly even outside of Germany.

The subject is explosive and problematical. It is problematical mainly because jazz dance has thus far eluded the strictures of scholarly analysis and definitions. The phenomenon of "jazz" is still miles ahead of any definitions that have been made of it.

The situation is further complicated by the fact that jazz dance has not been able to establish itself in the mind of the public as a distinct dance discipline. Whatever the reasons for this may be, one thing can clearly be read on the barometer of public opinion: it still has not broken through the sound barrier of prejudice (nightclub platitudes, cabaret garnishings, etc.). The general public usually reacts to body jazz with a helpless and embarassed shrug of the shoulders. To a certain extent the dancers themselves are responsible for this since they often escape to the dizzying heights of narcissistic ivory towers instead of launching a systematic information und publicity campaign. Yet, even though obscured by such complete lack of appreciation, neglected by the critics (with exceptions such as the dance historian Helmut Günther who early foresaw the trend here) and ridiculed by the fanatics of classical ballet, unnoticed in the chinks and crannies of the ballet establishment an entirely new consciousness of motion formed overnight.

In the process it very soon became evident that jazz dance in its original form can also be performed by untrained dancers and that it permits immediate experience and enjoyment of motion without imposing long preliminary periods of work and discipline.

Teachers, including those that have only a secondary interest in dance, rapidly recognized and began to utilize its considerable educational value for people of all ages and of all kinds. This ascendancy from the "unknown", particularly in the past ten years, has been accompanied by a number of negative side-effects. The countless stylistic aberrances that have sprung up in many places and the commercial value that quite obviously emanates from the concept "jazz dance" as an advertising factor are sufficient proof of this.

On the other hand, it is indisputable that the theater has been enlivened and given a more contemporary flavor by the gradually increasing presence of jazz dance on West German stages. The fact that dance academies, professional institutes and training centers have included jazz dance in their curricula is evidence of the degree of professional legitimacy it has already attained. However, let us not be deceived. The present activities, initiatives and approaches, as necessary and welcome as they may be, are in no way sufficient. New cells must be created, cultivated and intensively nourished.

Getting rid of narcissism in the dancers as well as lowering and overcoming the inhibition threshold in the amateur camp are an essential precondition.

In schools and universities, too, where dance

is not (voluntarily) included among the subjects taught, there is a lot of groundwork to be done. It is becoming more and more obvious that it is no longer enough just to train scientists, technologists, and computer specialists. Human beings can apparently only adequately comprehend concepts such as "quality of life", "prosperity", "leisure", or "freedom" if they are taught to do so from the start.

Achievement pressure, affluence-related neuroses and alienation, the acute problems of our times, can only be overcome with comprehensive artistic teaching programs in which dance, as a basic "personality event", assumes an especially important role.

Educational, cultural and financial policies that demonstrate insight, far-sight-edness and an ability to recognize early danger signs must intervene here constructively and purposefully. Only in this way can the processes that atrophy the human mind and soul be changed.

A balanced and reasoned redistribution of available means for this purpose would signify a courageous step in the direction of humanity. The concept "modern jazz dance" was consciously chosen since, in my work, I am concerned with a reconciliation and understanding between jazz dance and modern dance. Modern dance, often totally misused in utopian euphoria, can, through the vital light-heartedness and power of jazz, retrace its development to the origins of dance. Jazz dance on the other hand can, through the often bold experiments of modern dance, acquire new expressive and creative powers and thus venture into new areas of artistic expression.

Since there is, today, a multitude of styles both in modern dance and in jazz dance it seems to me necessary to present a spectrum of movement that is as neutral and as broadly distributed as possible. This, it seems to me, lays an initial foundation for technically correct and body-suited work.

In the exercise series "bar", "floor", "isolation" and "space", floor exercises form the largest contingent since I consider them of fundamental importance for conditioning the body. Particularly in the bar and floor series, I have included the influences, critically reflected, of my principle teacher of jazz, Frank Wagner, who is considered one of the leading North American experts in systematic jazz dance.

Elements of the Graham technique that are currently prominent in all areas of ballet activity and teaching are unmistakably present.

Technical jargon as a rule has been avoided in favor of more generally understandable wording. Such terms have been used only if they serve to clarify specific movements. The most important terms in general used today have been listed under "Dance Terminology".

In this book, I have attempted to exploit the experience and observations I have been able to accumulate in the past to develop an objective and open system of movements such that they might possibly serve as a "key" to distinctively motivated techniques.

It was not and is not possible to include all of the enormous amount of material on movement in the limits of the present volume.

I have attempted to make a harmonious choice of sequences which can condition the body for dance, i. e. jazz dance. The idea that less can sometimes be more seemed to me to be true in this case.

It cannot be overlooked that many of the exercises are of considerable therapeutic benefit and value. The profit gained from the exercise material presented is, of course, in the final analysis left to the initiative and responsibility of the individual.

Even if it is, at present, still difficult to define the phenomenon of jazz dance clearly and unmistakably in all of its dimensions, it seems to me to be all the more important to make a contribution in this direction by first of all attempting a didactic examination and organization of the available material on movement.

It has been my particular interest that the influence of this book go beyond a small circle of specialists and directly affect the public, initiating reflection and discussion of this subject in order to clear up misunderstandings and do away with legends that are still circulating.

Fred Traguth   Bonn, March, 1977

body placement	Body positioning.
coccyx	Lower extremity of the spinal column.
demi plié	Position in which legs are bent until the maximum tension on the Achilles tendon is reached without the heels leaving the floor.
développé	Development, leg movement.
grand plié	Position in which legs are bent to the maximum towards the floor. Heels leave the floor. This is true of all positions with the exception of the turned out second position. Here the heels are not raised from the floor in the grand plié.
gravitation	Gravity is used as a technical dance element.
passé	Carrying out, going through.
pelvis	Hip area.
relevé	Position in which heels are raised (weight on the balls of both feet).
thorax	Chest area.
torso	Pelvis and thorax together.

1

Bar Exercises

Work with the bar serves total body orienta-
tion. Using the bar as a partner is intended
to help support the balance and stabilization
of the center of the body.
The access to the "body ego" is greatly
facilitated in this way. As a rule, the dancer
begins his daily training with the bar in
order to tune the instruments of his body,
as it were. This is something like the
musician warming up with his instrument,
or the singer loosening up his voice.
The exercises shown on the following
pages are arranged in such a way as
to form a meaningful time sequence.
The centers of movement are primarily
the pelvis, the thorax area and the spinal
column, whose training is of central importance in modern jazz dance.
In general, a training class consists of
the classical time unit of 90 minutes which
is divided up as follows:
About 30–35 minutes at the bar, 10–15
minutes of in-place exercise and the remai-
ning 30–35 minutes in "free space".
Combinations such as floor isolation,
free space, etc. are also possible. The
important thing is that the training have
an underlying didactic strategy.

1f. Wrong: do not sag in the pelvis area as shown here (hollow back). On the contrary, pull the pelvis under the thorax. Stretch effect is heightened, body stability increased.

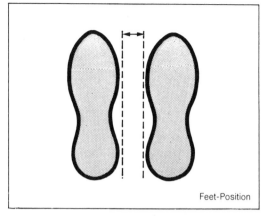

Feet-Position

1. Stretch: movement back and forth out of the arms accenting direction towards the bar. Important: stabilize the entire body and stretch in the vertical axis. Press the heels to the floor, straighten knees, thighs and the spinal column up to the back of the head; can be felt especially in the Achilles tendon, calf muscles and the pelvis area.
In the forward movement the elbows, which are bent, are *activ*. While the arms are being extended (pressing), the body remains in the diagonal position.

Leg and foot position: first parallel position (see note). Free choice of rhythm. Suggestion: 1 and 2 and 3 and 4 slowly, 6–8 times. Feel the body as a unit. Under no circumstances raise the heels from the floor. Do not force breathing – let the exercise do the breathing.

1f

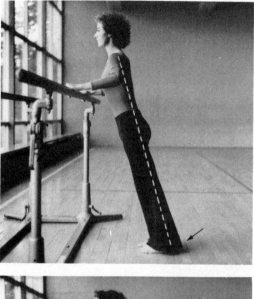
1

2. In principle like fig. 1: leg and foot position but now in the second parallel position (see note). Press heels to the floor while flexing body. Straighten knees, thighs, spinal column to the maximum. Pull pelvis under the thorax (contract). Here, too, feel the body as a unit and let the exercise do the breathing.

Note:

Leg and foot positions: the first parallel position, like the first turned out position, is always executed from the hip joint.
The legs and feet are not quite closed in the first parallel position. A distance of about 5 cm is maintained (see drawing). This increases the extension radius – especially with the body in a perpendicular position.
In the second turned out parallel position placement is also executed from the hip joint. Weight should always be evenly distributed on the soles of both feet. This rule applies to bar, floor, isolation and in-place exercises.

2

3. Torso should be as much as possible at right angles to the bar. Center of movement is the pelvis and base of spinal column.

Important: stretch the spinal column all the way up to the back of the head. Place arms at right angles to bar. The legs are kept straight, feet are parallel and almost closed.

3

4. Move torso slowly upward to a vertical position. All of back and arms are involved. Do not change body placement.

5. Feel the vertical position and stretching of the whole body. Do not raise shoulders. Keep neck loose. Let your body breathe.

3f. Wrong. Do not curve spinal column.

6

6. From this position bend knees (demi plié). Do not change torso and pelvis position.

7. Assume half-raised position. Knees remain in demi plié. Keep eyes looking straight ahead (horizontally). This helps maintain balance and body control.

8. In raised position (place weight on balls of feet) straighten knees. Feel the vertical position again and maintain balance.

9. Do not change body tension and slowly lower heels keeping legs straight.

7

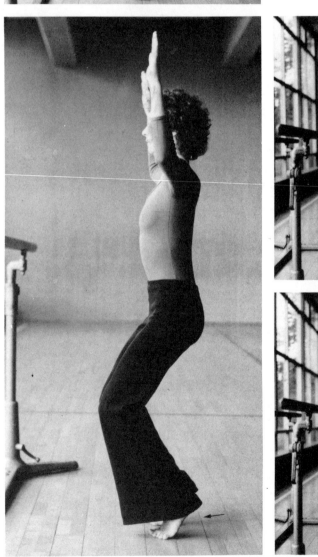

8

9

10. The exercise is now reversed. Do not change torso and arm positions. Move torso towards bar.

11. Key position has been reached. Positioning as in fig. 3.

12. The knees are again in demi plié. Center of movement is base of spinal column and pelvis. Important: Do not let ribs stick out. Keep heels on the floor.

13

13. Raise heels placing weight on balls of feet.

14

14. And now straighten legs. Body positioning does not change.

15

15. Keeping legs straight slowly lower heels to the floor; key position has been reached. Repeat about four times. Count from 1 to 8 in 2/4 time.

16. This sequence is a variation of exercise 2. Main difference is in leg and foot positioning. Initial position and body placement like in fig. 3. Moving legs from hips – this is important – turn feet outwards as far as possible to the first position. Be sure to place weight on outer edge of feet, keep legs straight.

16f. By no means do as is shown in the picture.

17. Slowly remove hands from the bar. No jerky movements. Pull the torso into the vertical axis in one slow and gliding motion. Do not raise shoulders and keep neck loose.

18

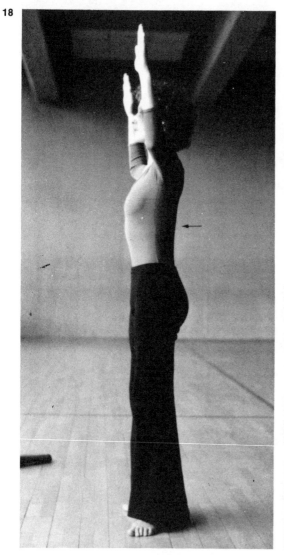

19

20

18. Feel the body as a unit in the vertical axis. Keep arms squared off, hands open. Stretch body from heels through pelvis and spinal column to head.

19. Holding this stretched position bend knees (demi plié). Keep heels on the floor.

20. Bend deeply (grand plié) raising heels. Do not change torso and arm positions. Maintain control of spinal column.

21. Slowly come up again, pressing heels to the floor. Maintain torso tension. Let breathing take care of itself.

21

22. Intermediate position: feet are kept turned out in first position, knees closed. Weight in this position is always on outer edge of feet.

23. Move torso back to bar in a gliding motion. Spine is kept straight. Feel center of movement in pelvis and spinal column.

24. Intermediate position as in fig. 16 (same principle). Maintain open first position.

22

23f. By no means do this.

23f

23

24

25f. Wrong and bad for the knees.

25. Continue in demi plié. Make sure that knees and torso stay in position.

26. Assume relevé (raised) position distributing weight evenly. Maintain a right angle at the junction of pelvis and spinal column.

27. Hold relevé. Continue holding turned out position (from the hips!). Straighten legs. Place torso at right angles to bar and rest of body. Leave rib cage relaxed. Let breathing come smoothly and by itself. Maximum tension has been reached. From here go back to initial position in fig. 16.

28f. Wrong. Compare torso, spine and arms with fig. 28.

28. Point of departure: base of spine and pelvis. Arms, elbows and head are important. Raise elbows upwards strongly. The back of the head should be an extension of the spinal column. Eyes are directed perpendicularly to the floor. This facilitates feeling for body placement.

29. Elbows together. Bend torso downwards from the hips (see fig. 28) stretching until elbows touch locked knees. Feet parallel.

30. Slowly extend torso, stretching the spinal column out from its base (important). Simultaneously raise head and arms.

31. Continue in extended position with knees locked. Slowly raise torso to vertical position without moving pelvis.

31f. Wrong. Never do this.

32.   Final position. Let breathing come by itself.
Feel the central axis in the entire body. Once again
correct placement of heels, knees, pelvis, spine,
torso, head and arms. Eyes straight ahead.
The main emphasis of this exercise is on extending
(stretching) the spinal column and, ultimately, stretching of the whole body.

32

33f. Wrong. Head and torso are not relaxed.

34f. Do not shift weight forward (towards bar) straining head and shoulders.

36f. Wrong. Pelvis out of position. Hands and head cramped. Defeats purpose of exercise.

37

33. Initial position: knees bent (demi plié), let head hang loosely. Hands opened and weight on fingertips. Smoothly executed knee-bends, a 1-2-3-4 rhythm is best.

34. Starting from center of body slowly straighten knees and spinal column. Keep head relaxed. Do not change hand position. Objective is stretching and extension of spinal column and legs. Do not try to touch knees with head. There is no need to exaggerate.

35. Basically as in fig. 33 except that thorax is twisted to the left or the right. Bend knees evenly in rhythm indicated in fig. 33. Important: counter tendency of pelvis to move out of position. Be sure to keep it in place.

38

36. Knees are slowly straightened, head relaxed, some weight on hands (i. e. fingers). Maintain twist, torso, pelvis positions.

37. Correct execution to the right side in demi plié position.

38. End of the exercise. Pelvis and torso twist to the right side.

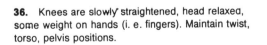

39. First phase: key position facing bar, second parallel position opened. Release (affected area: pelvis / spine). Spine has a slight convex curvature. These exercise require concentration and body sensitivity (see 39A as well).

40. Contract pelvis and lower spine (coccyx) as in fig. 39. Repeat about eight times to the rhythm contract-release, contract-release, etc. (see 40A).

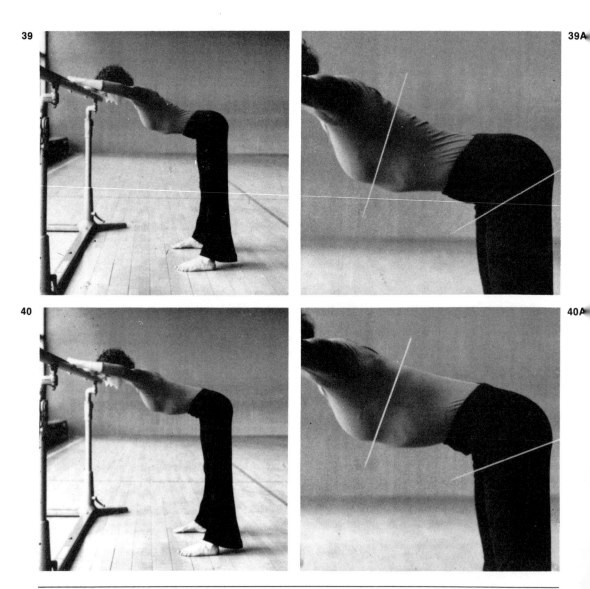

39   39A

40   40A

41. Second phase: Contract – release exercise as in fig. 39, but in demi plié. Do not change body and leg positions. Grip the bar loosely, keep arms parallel to each other and the torso. Although the center of movement in this very important exercise is primarily the middle of the body, the entire body is involved and "aware" (see 41A as well).

42. Contract only to the middle of the spine. Maintain straightness along body's central axis. This exercise isolates active and passive zones in the spinal column (see 42A as well).

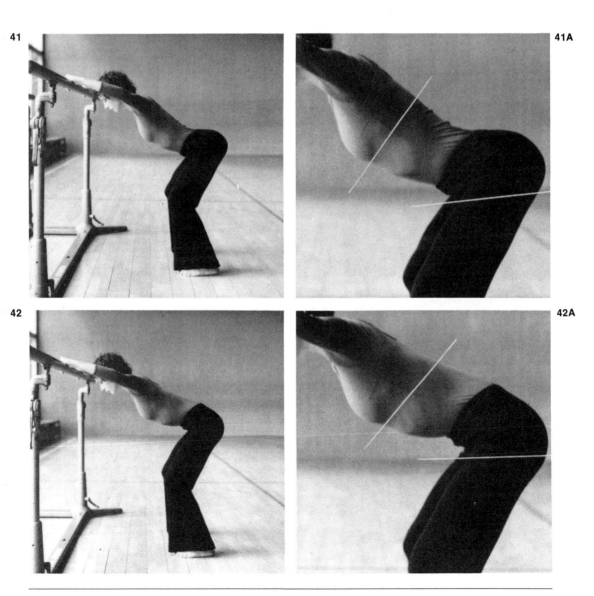

41   41A

42   42A

43. Third phase: demi plié relevé and release (see 43A).

44. Contract. Foot position is raised and parallel (see 44A).

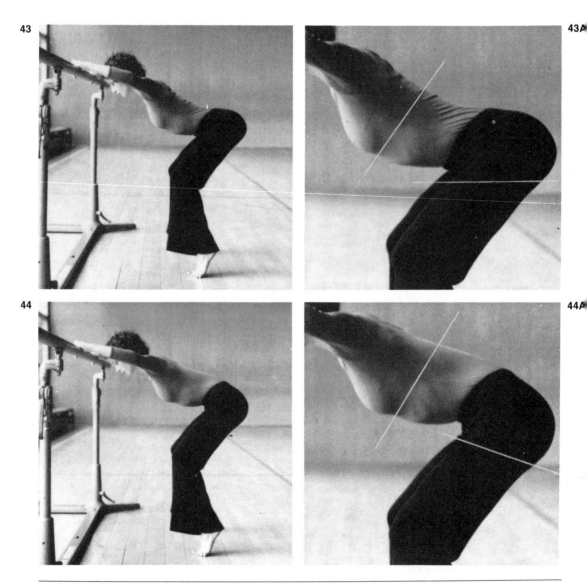

45. Fourth phase: Continue in raised position, straighten knees, release. Maintain squared off body position (see 45A).

46. Contract the middle of the spine again, and from the middle upwards, the spine stays isolated. Beginning of movement at angle forming point of pelvis. (see 46A)

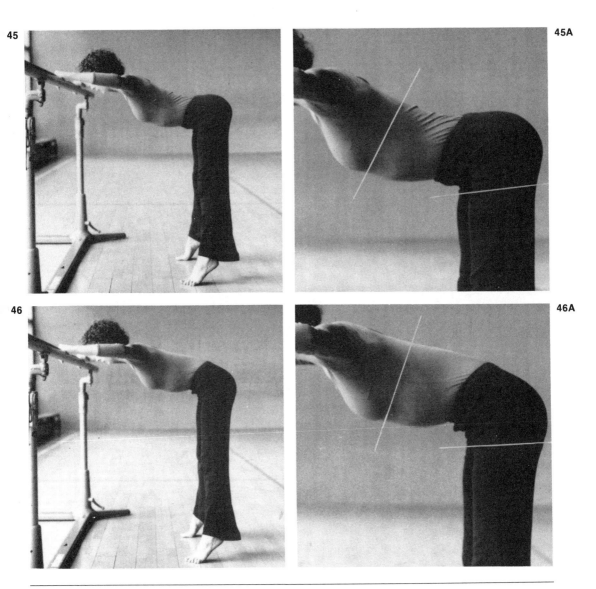

47. Fifth phase: basic position again. Second position parallel, at right angles to the bar, weight evenly distributed.

47

48. Sixth phase: maximum release of spinal column from spinal base to head. Assume demi plié position. Keep torso perpendicular.

48

49. Maximum contraction. Simultaneously straighten arms and legs, and go into raised position. End of this sequence.

This exercise primarily aims at training, strengthening and sensitivizing pelvis, spinal column and thorax.

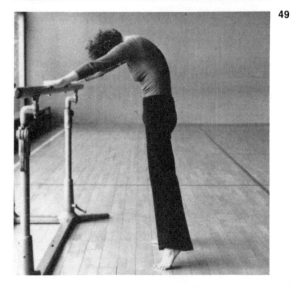

49

50f. Wrong.

50f

50. Initial position in demi plié and relevé (raised) at right angles to bar. Body positioning as in the previous sequences.

50

51. Lean torso back in a diagonal line away from bar (not a back bend!). Maintain relevé. Important: from a continuous straight line running from knees through thighs, pelvis, spinal column to head. Stiffen abdominal and gluteal muscles. Keep thighs stiff.

52. Slowly remove hands from bar as shown in the illustration. Keep balance. Eyes straight ahead.

53. From fig. 52 back to original position. Repeat about 4 times. Character and rhythm of movement – staccato-like.

54

55

56

57

54. Starting position: heels raised, knees locked. Hold on to bar lightly. Distribute weight evenly on both feet. Stretch torso and spinal column. Bend elbows slightly.

55. Beginning by tipping pelvis backwards (release). Keep heels raised during the exercise.

56. Pull pelvis in under torso (contract) and at same time slowly go into a demi plié.

57. From demi plié continue with a gliding motion to the floor and simultaneously release pelvis (pelvis movement is also gliding).

58

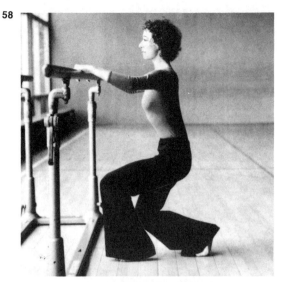

58. Contract pelvis again, continuing in grand plié. Keep heels raised and maintain axis through center of body. Keep hands loosely on the bar.

59

59. Right (or left) knee touches the floor while pelvis goes into release. Left (or right) heel remains raised. Extend (stretch and lift) torso from center of body.
End of exercise in grand plié.

60

60. With right knee still on the floor contract pelvis back in under rest of torso. Do the exercise in reverse, i. e. from grand plié through demi plié back to erect positions with legs straight and knees locked, keeping heels raised at all times and alternating contract and release positions of the pelvis.

Torso / Twist / Stretch

61. Starting position (without bar). Second position
opened normally (from the hips). Concentrate on
the center axis. From here . . .

61

62

62. . . . slowly lift torso up pulling it over to the right in a wide circular motion. Important: do not lose control on the right side, bending in and yielding in the pelvis. The movement originates in the pelvis and is executed describing as wide a circle as possible (stretch).

63

63. Maximum tension in the sideways positions has been reached. Keep pelvis steady, do not yield. Knees remain locked.

64

64. Torso slowly turns in a twist. Left side of pelvis and leg follow like a screw being turned to the right against resistance. Keep knees stiff. Arms turn with torso.

65f

65f. ... By no means do this. Arms must not hang downwards. On the contrary they should be extended horizontally at the same angle as the torso with the hands held together (see fig. 65). Left leg and left half of pelvis must not remain turned out. They must turn in (to the right) with the rest of the body.

65. Hands are held together. Arms extended. Torso, left half of pelvis and left leg are as much as possible in the pelvis-thorax axis. Twist. Left heel is pressed to the floor. Spinal column is extended.

65

66. Turn the screw slowly back to the left. Twist torso between extended arms. Left leg and side of pelvis turn with the motion. Knees remain locked and heels on the floor. Reverse twist.

67. Torso twist is completed.'Torso stretch emanates from the pelvis. Pull torso upwards in a wide circle. Legs and feet in open second position. Do not move pelvis. Imagine it is fastened in a vice so it cannot give way.

68. Hands and arms separate while torso returns to vertical position.

69. Final position or initial position for the other side. Do exercise alternately, twice for both sides. The exercise consists of two phases. First phase: count from 1–8 from initial position to the end of the twist. Second phase: count from 1–8 while returning to the initial position. Breathing: concentrate on exhaling, let inhaling come by itself (do not force it).

70. Demi plié (press heels to the floor), first position, open. Hands, i. e. fingers on the floor. Torso and head bent forward, relaxed.

71. From the front. Head and neck are relaxed.

70A. Initial position in profile. Place weight on the outer edges of the feet. Push knees back (towards wall), feel leverage in arms and knees.

71A. Extend legs slowly in 4 stages (first position turned out); simultaneously extend spinal column out from the pelvis. Head relaxed. Weight on fingertips and outer edges of feet. Press insides of thighs firmly together. By no means try to touch knees with head. It is important that the body be in good functional working order.

72. First position open (without bar). Arms squared off. Pelvis and torso form one block. Establish a center axis from the heels to the head. Eyes to the front. Face and neck relaxed.

73. First phase: move pelvis to the right. It is important that the body remain vertically stable. Only the pelvis moves.

74. Move pelvis to the left. Knees are kept straight, hands are opened as extensions of the forearms.

75. Same process starting to the left. Keep arms squared off. Pelvis and head shift while torso stays in place forming a figure-S.

75

76

79

77

76. Third phase: To the right again. Head not involved. Demi plié with right leg while left leg assumes relevé position (weight on ball of foot).

77. The same in reverse. Torso remains vertical. Extend spinal column.

78. Fourth phase: Head included again. Five centers of movement are involved:
1. Relevé with the right foot.
2. Demi plié with both knees.
3. Pelvis pulled to the left as far as possible.
4. Head inclined to the left.
5. Elbows bent at right angles.

79. The movement carried out to the right. From the pelvis-head isolation we have arrived at isolations involving the whole body. Repeat every phase about 4 times for both sides of body.

78

80. First phase: Initial position: Place right (or left) leg on the bar. Weight on the middle of foot on bar. Firm grip on the bar. Both legs are in parallel position. Right knee sharply bent, the other straight. Spinal column, as is clearly shown in the photograph, is extended (stretched) in a straight line from the coccyx to the back of the head.

81. In slow motion move torso forwards towards the bar (firmly gripping bar) and at the same time extend right leg.

82

82. Continue moving torso (do not overstrain) until chest touches knee. Stretch spinal column and both legs to the maximum.

83

83. Continue by going into demi plié. Both legs remain parallel. Keep head and neck relaxed.

84

84. Second phase: Repeat the exercise with the supporting leg in relevé, knee locked, spinal column stretched out even farther.

85. Again extend torso forward from the center of the body towards the bar. Maintain relevé during entire exercise.

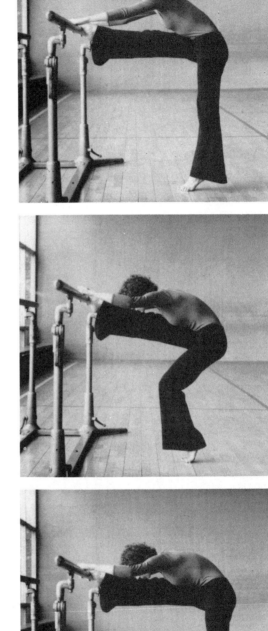

85

86. Holding relevé go into demi plié. Thorax touches leg again. Pull torso over right leg towards bar.

86

87. In this very tense position slowly extend weight-bearing leg maintaining relevé. Keep head relaxed. Let breathing take care of itself.
Pause shortly and then continue with the other side.
Repeat twice for each side.

87

88. Begin with back to bar. First position parallel. Raise right (or left) leg in a passé. Support leg remains straight during the exercise, as do torso and spine. Do not let pelvis sag. On the contrary concentrate on lifting it. Grip bar tightly.

89. Extend leg forward at an angle of 90 degrees. Keep support leg steady.

90. From the first position parallel raise right leg
again in a passé but with heel flexed.

91

91. When leg is fully extended, bend back from pelvis. In doing so let hands slide sideways down the bar. Maintain flex and weight of leg. Support leg is stretched, heel firmly on the floor.

92. Repeat exercise, but with support leg in relevé. It is best to do the exercise twice on both sides – twice without relevé and twice with heel raised. Beginners are advised to work with a partner. A maximum of body expansion can be attained with this exercise.

92

93. Starting position: With back to the bar in first position parallel. Body placement: stretch knees, torso, spinal column and be aware of them. Do not forget to stretch neck as well.

94. From starting position go into grand plié (feet parallel and closed), heels raised. Torso remains extended. When correctly executed body feels light.

95. From here press heels to the floor. At the same time thrust pelvis forward under the thorax and bend back in a wide circle from the pelvis. Arms are loosely extended and slide apart sideways on the bar. At the end of the movement the knees are straight and stretched.

96. After this rise vertically in relevé. Feel vertical position. Develop power from center of body (pelvis-thorax). Repeat about 4 times with an impulsive rhythm. This exercise is especially good for strengthening the back which is of singular importance in every dancing technique.

93

95

94

96

97. Initial position: Legs are opened wide and parallel in the fourth position. Body "hangs" extended from the bar. Arms, legs, spine are stretched out straight. Grip bar firmly. Tip of right foot touches floor. From here . . .

98. . . . strongly contract pelvis. In doing so right leg is slowly pulled forward by the tension until . . .

99. . . . the end of the exercise has been reached. Right knee is pulled up under left leg and bears a slight amount of weight. Hold pelvis contraction. Now start release in pelvis. Slowly extend leg again and return to initial position (fig. 97). Repeat 4 times for each side. Execute slowly.

This exercise gives the body a great deal of stretching.

97

99

98

100.   First phase: Initial position: legs are parallel. Support leg in demi plié. Other leg raised from hip joint. Spine strongly curved out. From here . . .

101.   . . . swing raised leg straight back keeping it parallel (foot extended). At the same time extend torso (spinal column) forward. Back of head is part of spinal column. Support leg is in demi plié. Body reclines horizontally in space. Grip bar loosely. From here back to the initial position and repeat. Exercise concentrates on center of pelvis. Repeat 8 times for either side using the rhythm 1 and 2 and 1 and . . . etc.

102.   Second phase: Support leg extended in relevé. If possible head and knee touch (strongly curve spine). This increases tension. Then . . .

103.   . . . again swing raised leg straight back keeping it parallel but this time bend both knees sharply. Support leg remains in relevé. Stretch out spinal column. Concentrate on thigh of lifted leg. It should form part of a straight line running through spine to head. Grip bar firmly. Repeat 8 times for each side in a 1 and 2 rhythm.

100

101

102

103

104. Initial position: Stand in second position with side to the bar and gripping bar tightly. Contract pelvis (here to the left). Shift weight to left and go into demi plié. Left foot goes into relevé. Plenty of weight on the ball of the foot. Right leg is straight. Center of gravity is center of pelvis.

105. Pull pelvis to the left in a release and extend left leg loosely until heel leaves the floor. Right foot remains flat on the floor. Important: Do not move pelvis backwards. Movement is from side to side. Thorax is partly involved.

106. Contract pelvis in under thorax. Slowly shift weight to the right. Right leg goes into demi plié while left arm is raised. Do not raise shoulders. Feel tension in pelvis.

107. Continue to contract pelvis towards bar until left leg comes up in a passé. Simultaneously extend left side of torso. From here . . .

108. . . . release pelvis and swing left leg out to
the side at the same time rising up in a relevé. Hold
bar lightly so as not to lose balance.
About 4 times for either side. Contract slowly, release
slowly with ensuing delay.

108

2

Floor Exercises

The following floor exercises, like the bar
exercises, were chosen to fit into the esta-
blished overall time structure. Most of the
exercises illustrated here are so-called
simultaneous exercises. This means that
when an exercise is being executed that
concentrates on a movement in a certain
area, other centers of movement are created in the body at the same time.

The body's mobility and its capacity for
expansion can be increased by using this
principle and the resistance of the floor.
Flexibility and heightened body feeling
are consciously developed through detai-
led training, especially in the torso area,
which is intensified by the "floor technique". Body awareness increases and
consciousness of the dialectic of tension
and relaxation grows.

1. First phase: Sit in first position turned out in demi plié. Center of body is middle of pelvis. Soles of feet are together. Grip ankles. With this exercise the torso can be stretched out ot the center. Back rounded. Raise elbows up away from knees while torso is lightly pressed down towards floor. Press knees to the floor at the same time. Pressure causes expansion in the thorax, pelvis and thighs. In this excrcise movement emanates from the coccyx.

1

2. Second phase: After the first phase has been completed using a 1–8 count start from coccyx again continuing to grip ankles with hands. Strengthens initial movement. Feel leverage in arms and elbows. Head is relaxed. Back is rounded as much as possible. Count to 4 . . .

3. Third phase: . . . then on 5 begin to stretch out the spinal column starting from the coccyx. Simultaneously activate knees, elbows, arms, hands and soles of feet. Do not raise shoulders.

3f. By no means do this.

4. Fourth phase: Continue counting to 8 – slowly
– extending the spinal column from the coccyx on
up to the last neck vertebra. Imagine you are going
up the spinal column like a ladder. Thorax area stret-
ches forward. End of exercise. Repeat 4 times. Carry
out smoothly.

4

5. Basic position: Sit in first position turned out in demi plié. Lift up entire thorax area and stretch spinal column. Lock hands behind head and open elbows as far as possible out to the side. Turn knees outward moving legs from hip joint. Soles of feet together. Knees push down towards the floor so that a simultaneous tension is created in the body.

6. In this position twist thorax. Close elbows. Shoulders are actively involved. Do not change vertical axis in the twist position.

7. In twist position thorax moves forward to knee, elbows closed, such that right elbow touches left knee. Strongly tense the right half of thorax.

8. Twist right to center position. Elbows remain closed. Spine is rounded and upper thorax area actively involved.

8

9. Twist to right keeping elbows closed so that the left half of thorax is activated (easily recognizable in the picture). Left elbow touches right knee, spinal column kept rounded.

9

10. Stretch out spinal column from coccyx. Maintain twist. Elbows remain closed. Whole thorax area is active.

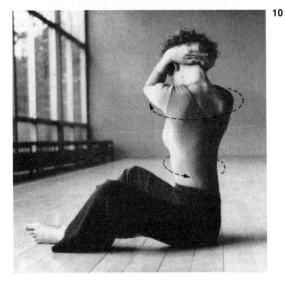

10

11. Maintain position. Extend elbows as far as they will go. Do not raise shoulders. Maximum thorax-twist tension.

11

12. From twist to right return to basic position. Feel thoryx lift. Begin exercise in the other direction. Repeat twice for both sides alternating sides. Exercise has 8 phases. Count every phase such that there is a slow count of 1–8.

12

13. Initial postion: Again in first position turned out in demi plié. Extend thorax from body center while pulling it down towards the floor. Feel rounding of spinal column, elbows are closed and touching heels. Simultaneously establish tension in pelvis and leg area.

14. Initiate movement in coccyx. Extend spinal column upward against resistance. Upper thorax area remains rounded and elbows together.

13

14

15. Continue extending spinal column moving thorax back into diagonal position. Pelvis and abdominal muscles now begin to contract. Elbows remain together. Shoulders are actively affected.

16. Now begin with pelvis release so that spinal column and thorax extend in a straight diagonal line. Abdominal muscles are active. Elbows spread as far as possible. Hands locked behind head.

17. Maintain thorax and pelvis tension and return to vertical initial position. Repeat 4 times with a count of 1–4.

18. Initial position: First position, parallel and extended. Extend spinal column vertically from coccyx. Place weight on hands on either side (fingers spread) thus facilitating lift in thoryx area. Extend legs and feet (backs of knees flat on the floor). Eyes to the front, lift in head and neck.

19. Maintain placement, flex feet, knees locked. Feel soles of feet as a surface. Flex feet again. Repeat 4 times.

20. Go on to second phase. Flex feet and simultaneously go into demi plié. There are now three centers: ankles, knees and hips. Keep pelvis steady. Maintain spinal column and thorax in lift.

21. Extend legs and feet to the maximum. Hands as props, elbows slightly bent. Aids in lifting thorax and extending spinal column. Repeat 4 times.

22

22. Initial position: Basically like exercise 4, Fig. 19 except that now arms are extended forward horizontally. Palms open and upward.

23. First phase: Extend thorax from pelvis center slowly out over legs. Begin extending from coccyx. Arms and hands are actively involved in the exercise.

24. This phase ends on 8 (count of 1–8) at which point firmly grip feet. Stretch legs and thorax as far forward as possible. Head touches knees. Delay this a little. It intensifies the expansion effect.

25. Third phase (four parts): Spinal column extends up out of coccyx. Grip feet, arms stretch simultaneously. Center of movement is pelvis and lower thorax area. Count of 4.

23

24

25

26. Fourth phase: On the count of 5 extend spinal column in pelvis area. Grip feet. Elbows are slightly bent. Count to 8 and . . .

27. . . . let got, spine remains extended, thorax lifts . . .

28. . . . slowly up and returns to vertical initial position. Do not raise shoulders. Do not holf breath. Exhale. Every phase has a count of 1–8. Third and fourth phases are divided into 2 times 4. Repeat exercise 4 times.

29. Initial position: Thorax lift in vertical axis, shoulders pulled down, arms raised and slightly rounded. Legs in demi plié and parallel. Pressure on feet so that calf muscles come into play. Eyes straight ahead.

29

30. First phase (count of 1–4): Begin contracting pelvis. Simultaneously extend legs letting feet slide on floor. Move arms to horizontally extended position. Spinal column extends back and abdominal muscles become active.

30

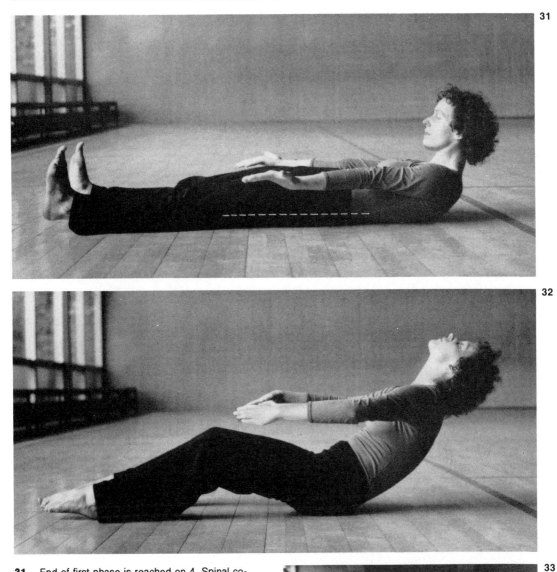

31. End of first phase is reached on 4. Spinal column, pelvis, back of knees pressed flat to floor (feel
the pressure). Head stays up, eyes ahead. Stomach
muscles are tensed. Feet flexed. Breathe smoothly.

32. Second phase (count 1–4): All movements
begin simultaneously: Bend head back (eyes on
ceiling), bend knees slowly, extend feet and slide,
raise arms, abdominal muscles active. While thorax
is rising there is release in pelvis.

33. Initial position reached again. Repeat 4 times.

34

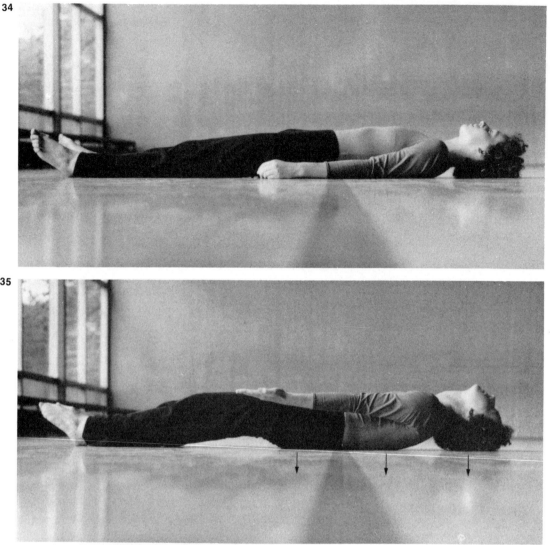

35

36

34. First phase: Completely relax body and exhale. Inhalation will come by itself.

35. Tension: Contract pelvis. Press pelvis to the floor and be aware of the pressure. At the same time head back and knees slightly bent. Bring abdominal muscles into play. Forceful exhalation while contracting. Hold tension about 5 seconds then relax abruptly and let breathing come by itself. Repeat 4 times.

36. Second phase: Completely relax again. Breathe in deeply and slowly.

37. Stretch body and flex. Legs parallel. Tension goes from head through whole body to the tips of toes. Body is flat on floor.

38. Raise pelvis and thorax area up in an arch. Knees are locked. There is weight on heels, arms and shoulder blades. Release, drop down gently, relax. Repeat about 4–6 times. No specific count.

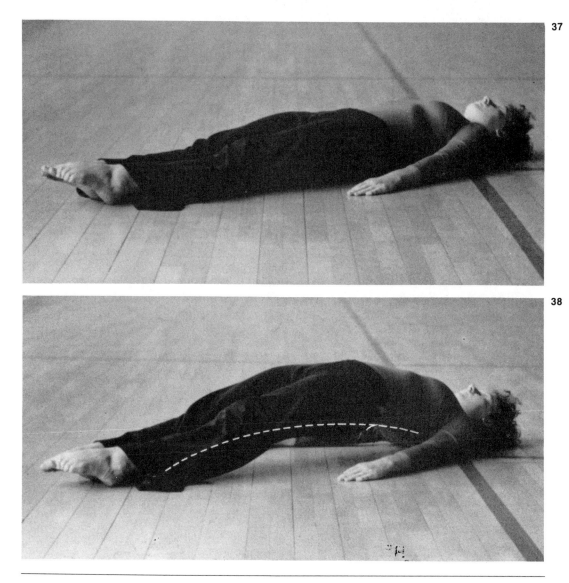

37

38

39. Third phase: Grip ankles. Knees are sharply bent, legs parallel. Consciously press pelvis and spinal column down into the floor. Then, as shown here, forcefully lift pelvis and thorax up towards ceiling. There is pressure on shoulder blades. Keep hands on ankles. Feet raise up in relevé. Repeat 2–3 times.

40. Fourth phase: Basically like Fig. 39 except body works without support. Hold arms up vertically and again raise pelvis, thorax, heels (weight on balls of feet) up as high as possible.

40

41. First phase: Stretch out flat on floor. Grip right knee and bend it back pressing back and pelvis into the floor and extending lift as far as possible.

42. Second phase: Now alternately left and right. Extended leg and thorax rise slightly from the floor. Head and knee touch. Maintain grip on knee.

41

42

43

44

43. Third phase: Right foot flexed, hands grip bottom of foot in the middle, knee touches chest, left leg thoroughly extended. Spinal column and pelvis stay on the floor during this phase.

44. Slowly extend leg and start to stretch without changing body position. Exercise offers a maximum of stretch. Execute slowly. Repeat twice for both sides.

45. Starting position: Second position turned out opened wide. Legs and feet extended (backs of knees pressed to the floor). Hands support on either side (fingertips). Lift thorax from pelvis center. Stretch spinal column from coccyx to neck vertebrae. Elbows are bent slightly. Do not raise shoulders. Eyes ahead. Keep body placement under control.

46. First phase: Hold arms out to either side parallel to leg position. Hold lift and activate side muscles.

46A. Second position in side view. Concentrate on arms and spine. Arms are slightly rounded and slightly bent at the elbow.

47. Second phase: Hands grip backs of knees from inside of leg. Simultaneously leg in demi plié, feet flexed, maintain thorax lift.

47A. Concentrate on spine and thorax. Hold simultaneous tension.

48

48A

49

50

48. Third phase: Straighten legs, continue with
thorax lift and hands on knees, feet are flexed.

48A. Extend flexed feet. Consciously feel stretch
in spinal column and simultaneous tension in body.
Repeat 4 times in 2/4 time.

49. Fourth phase: Raise arms with the flat of the
palms turned to the front. Do not raise shoulders.
Open legs as far as possible in second position
and turn out. Lift up in the thorax area.

50. Do not change body placement. Slowly move
thorax ahead at an angle. Spinal column remains
stretched. Hold leg and pelvis tension.

51. Flex feet and knees. Control movement centers
such as feet, knees, pelvis, hip joints and thorax.
From here slowly simultaneously stretch returning
to initial position (see Fig. 49). Repeat 4 times to
a slow count.

51

52. Fifth phase: Maintaining initial position and initial tension, twist thorax sharply to the left. Hands used as support (elbows slightly bent) to facilitate lift in thorax. Twist vigorously around spinal column which must remain absolutely vertical.

53f. Wrong. Do not let thorax sag and bend spine.

53. Sharp twist to the right. Hands give simultaneous support. Maintain center axis. Repeat 4 times. Best rhythm is 3/4 time: twist on 1 and rest on 2 and 3.

54. Sixth phase: From initial position again twist thorax strongly to the right. Simultaneously flex legs, feet and arms. Concentrate on keeping spinal column vertical. Do not raise shoulders. Keep neck relaxed, legs turned out.

55f. Wrong. Compare thorax, arms and head.

55. Same process to the left. The effect of the sequence is added to by the accompanying simultaneous movements and tensions. Repeat 4 times on both sides in 3/4 time.

54

55f

55

56. Initial position: Spread legs as far as possible in second position turned out. Extend legs and feet as far as possible. Press thighs to the floor and keep them there. Some weight on forearms. Bend thorax forward letting head hang loosely. Maintain this position and get body adjusted. Breathe deeply and smoothly.

57. Head remains on floor. Maintain turned out second position.

56A. Extend elbows to the side (hands on top of each other) such that forearms are flat on the floor. Bend thorax forward until forehead touches floor (if possible). Intensify leg stretch. Continue to breathe smoothly.

57A. First phase: No change in thorax area, knees and feet are flexed.

58. Second phase: Place forearms parallel again and place weight on them. With the pressure thus generated begin spinal stretch in coccyx. Thorax is at this point as parallel to floor as possible.

56A

59

57A

60

58

59. Arms leave the floor (elbows remain bent). Thorax is moved up in a gliding motion. Maintain leg extension.

60. Third phase: Thorax, spine and head are extended. Arms remain squared off to the front.

61

62

61. Head is bent back and forth (isolated) without any change in body tension.

62. Flex feet when head is bent back. Extend when bent forward. Body remains stable.

63. Flex feet and knees simultaneously. Body and arm placement remain unchanged.

63A. Hold thorax in vertical position and fix eyes on ceiling. The exercise is multipurpose. Movement centers affected: head, arms, elbows, thorax, hip joints, knees, feet and legs in longitudinal turn. Repeat each phase 4 times, preferably in 2/4 time.

63

63A

64. Initial position: Second position turned out as in fig. 45, exercise 9.

64

65. Contract in pelvis. Simultaneously flex feet, extend arms forward and absorb contraction tension – legs remain extended, knees locked.

65

66. Going with contraction and moving head and thorax straight out over floor extend spinal column diagonally forward. Arms are extended to either side such that feet are touched lightly adding to thoryx tension. From here return to initial position in a gliding and lifting movement. Repeat exercise 4 times in 3/4 time. Contract on 1, pause on 2 and 3.

66

67. Initial position: Again second position turned out. Posture and placement just like in fig. 45, exercise 9.

68. First phase: Pull thorax over horizontally to the right. Arms remain extended. Do not bend thorax. The whole side is stretched more or less like a rubber band . . .

69. . . . and now to the left . . .

70. . . . to the right again flexing left foot . . .

71. . . . thorax to the left simultaneously flexing right foot.

72. Third phase: Thorax to the right simultaneously flexing left foot and leg . . .

73. . . . same process on other side. Make sure that the exercise is executed in countermovement, i. e. when thorax moves left the left leg is extended and only the right leg is flexed. Isolate body. Repeat every phase 4 times in 2/4 time.

74

75

76

74. Initial position: Second position turned out. Thorax is bent over right leg. Grip middle of foot with right hand and hold on firmly during exercise. Left hand presses thigh to floor just below hip joint. Thorax is turned and head relaxed. Execute twist in three phases . . .

75. . . . left elbow is pulled back . . .

76. . . . left shoulder follows. Hands remain in their supporting positions . . .

77. . . . in a kind of echo effect thorax follows elbow and shoulder movement turning left up out to center of body. Head follows through and eyes are raised. Right arm is stretched and hand lightly grips middle of foot. This increases thorax twist.

78. Carry out in reserve. Turn thorax back. Left shoulder pushes forward, elbow follows, thorax slowly returns to initial position. Do exercise slowly so as to execute every phase carefully and correctly. Repeat 4 times.

77

78

79. Initial position: Second position turned out. Thorax along with left arm sharply bent over to the right side. Firmly grip middle of right foot with right hand. Keep head relaxed, both thighs pressed to the floor.

80. Turn thorax in until it is bent over right leg. Both hands (crossed) grip middle of foot. Maintain second position turned out.

81. Slowly bend both knees so that tension diminishes. The left leg turns in at the hip joint. Keep hands in position. Thorax lies relaxed over bent right knee.

82f. Wrong. Do not turn leg in from thigh.

82. Slowly go into twist again. Begin movement with left leg. Extend until second position turned out is reached again. Left thigh must touch floor. Maintain grip and twist thorax under arms. Repeat twice on both sides.

81

82f

82

83

83. Initial position: Second position turned out.

84. Raise right leg with slightly bouncing movement. Thorax moves back a little. Abdominal muscles are brought into play. Simultaneously right arm moves away to the right while left arm moves forward parallel to right leg.

85. Right leg is swung over to left leg forming first position parallel. At the same time thorax is bent over extended leg (chest touches knees). Hands grip middle of feet, head relaxed. From this position . . .

84f. Wrong. Do not leave arms extending directly away from sides. Do not let thorax sag. This costs energy.

84

84f

85

86. . . . repeat the exercise from left to right. Mind thorax, arms and stomach muscles. Extend legs and feet . . .

87. . . . and again vigorously go into first position parallel. Body placement is (front view) diagonal.

88. Same exercise again but now simultaneously bend knee and foot in a flex. While extending leg and foot swing leg into first position parallel as in fig. 85 . . .

89. . . . and repeat exercise from left to right. Repeat every phase of exercise twice for each side.

90.   From second position turned out (see fig. 83) execute a strong twist to the left with the entire torso. Extended leg follows through such that the inner edge of foot touches the floor. Square arms off and support weight of torso on fingertips (spread). Stretch leg and spine out straight . . .

91.   . . . then swing lightly past the second position executing a torso twist to the right. From center of body twist vigorously around center axis. Left leg (extended) — clearly visible in the photograph — follows through from hip, turning until the inner edge of foot touches floor. Hands continue to support torso.

92.   Execute a torso twist once again to the left and simultaneously bend both knees (fourth position) . . .

93.   . . . and again passing second position with a flowing motion (extending legs in the process) execute a torso twist to the right with legs in plié. Repeat each phase of exercise (extended and plié) 4 times.

90

92

91

93

94. Start in fourth position: Bend both knees. Center of gravity in the middle. Stretch spinal column. Raise head and hold arms out to either side.

94

95. Execute torso twist to left. Steady twisting movement around spinal column. Arms are turned out and held slanted diagonally downward.

95

96. Twist to the right. Arms are turned in and hands are closed to form fists. Place considerable weight on left foot until heel and knee rise slightly from the floor. This takes place simultaneously, i. e. when torso twist (from left to right) initiates. Repeat exercise 4 times for each side in slow 2/4 time.

96

97. Initial position: Fourth position, placement as in fig. 94. Center point is pelvis on which weight is evenly distributed.

98. Lay thorax forward across bent (left) leg. Forearms are laid flat on the floor. Forehead touches floor. Important: Pull thorax forward out of center.

99. From this position slowly extend right leg. Inner edge of right foot and heel glide across the floor during extension (so-called arabesque). Important: Maintain countertension in right half of thorax while leg is being extended. Repeat exercise 4 times on either side. No specific rhythm.

97

98

99

100

101

100. Initial position: Fourth position, placement as in fig. 94.

101. Lift bent left leg from floor, simultaneously raising arms to form a circle around head. Move thorax back slightly and activate abdominal muscles. Do not move shoulders up. Relax neck, eyes ahead.

102. Now extend lefted leg simultaneously extending arms to either side. Tense thorax and abdominal muscles. Head up, neck relaxed. Let breathing come naturally.

103. Move thorax back farther turning arms and lowering them such that they touch the floor. Arms glide slowly back to a diagonal position. Left leg remains suspended in the air. Abdominal muscles are activated.

104. Continue gliding until thorax is on floor. Right knee and thigh are raised slightly from the floor. Foot remains on floor, however. Important: Press thorax and pelvis area to the floor as much as possible. Left leg remains lifted and extended. From here . . .

105. . . . simultaneously bend arms, thorax, leg in a rapid movement back to position in fig. 101 and from there return to fourth position. Exercise requires strength in torso region. Repeat twice on either side using any suitable rhythm. Important: Do not hold breath. Make sure to exhale.

105

106

107

106. Initial position: Extend thorax forward from fourth position keeping it as parallel to floor as possible. Extend spinal column and reach out with arms on either side.

107. Right arm leads this phase of movement. With left arm prop up thorax. Right knee is pressed to the floor.

107A. Propping thorax up with left forearm, begin cutting movement backwards keeping right arm above and parallel to floor.

108. Arm continues, thorax follows through, touching floor, left shoulder rolling up gently.

109. Keep as flat on the floor as possible using left forearm as a prop and then left shoulder roll will take care of itself. Press right knee to floor as far as possible.

109A. Continue spiral movement with right arm in direction of right foot. Head follows movement, thorax is pressed to floor.

109

110

110. Final phase: Right hand touches right foot. Right knee is raised from floor (foot remains extended!). Head follows in direction of movement. Left arm is passive.

110A. Press thorax, spinal column and pelvis to floor as much as possible.

111. Take spiral back to initial position. Right hand moves just above floor, left shoulder rolls up and left forearm supports. Extend thorax until initial position has been reached. Repeat 4 times for either side with any suitable rhythm.

110A

111

112. Initial position: Lie flat on back, arms and
legs squared off. With a rolling motion . . .

113. . . . move torso to left until right leg is extended to right. Arms reach out simultaneously. Execute in one continuous motion: roll, assume stance, extend torso parallel to floor, roll back again over left side.

114. Roll to right (across shoulder blades). Extend left leg far to left in roll. Place weight on right lower leg. When beginning roll, bend torso forward, pull arms in. Bend elbows and repeat to left. Repeat 4 times in smooth rhythm.

113

114

115. Start again with fourth position. Mind body placement (see fig 94). Arms are held out. Breathe evenly during exercise.

116. Lift right knee (behind body) off of floor slightly, extend lower leg and foot. Keep thorax stretched.

117. Extend raised right lower leg to right (parallel, not turned out) left arm moves simultaneously forward. Right thorax region is activated. From this position swing extended right leg . . .

118. . . . back to right and side-roll into back across left sholuder blade. Transitional phase as in photograph with arms extended and back on floor for a moment. Legs and foot are extended in second position.

119. Roll continues on right shoulder and right side of torso. Right knee is bent, right forearm helps to push up into upright position.

120. Roll ends with left leg extended. Both arms to right side, and parallel to leg.

121. Then with light pressure on both thighs lift pelvis up. Simultaneously extend thorax upwards placing weight on right thigh. Flex left heel, stretch out arms opening hands and spreading fingers as far as possible. Continue stretching and . . .

122. . . . then come down on both thighs. Right knee slides back a little. Thorax and arm tension is maintained. Leave left leg fully extended. Keep heel flexed and with a slightly bouncing motion pull thorax out over extended leg (about 8 times). After a short pause repeat on other side.
Execute on either side using 8 times the 1–2 beat.

123. Initial position: Basically as in fourth position. Right leg stretched with heel flexed, arms raised and rounded. Both thighs are pressed to floor. Neck and shoulders are relaxed. Then . . .

123

124. . . . pulling thorax forward out of pelvis move arms over flexed heel. Initiate extension of spinal column in coccyx. Press thighs to floor. Eyes look straight ahead.

125. In this position twist to right using hands for support. Bend elbows slightly. Turn torso as far around as possible maintaining leg position. Keep turning . . .

124

125

126. . . . until legs are together. Pelvis is pressed down on floor. Thorax is bent up, arms extended (do not raise shoulders up), hands flat on floor for support. Continue twist spiral . . .

127. . . . by swinging right leg over extended left leg and returning to initial position on other side. Repeat 4 times for either side at a smooth pace.

128. Start with first position parallel, legs and feet extended, thorax pulled forward . . .

129. Fall back with thorax bending both legs as shown in picture. Arms and hands are pressed on floor.

130. With a rapid movement extend right leg straight up towards ceiling. Entire thorax lifts off floor. Stretch spine; press arms down on floor. This facilitates lift. Left foot is evenly weighted. From here return to position in fig. 129 and then, stretching legs and raising thorax, simultaneously regain initial position.

131. Repeat exercise in all phases. In thorax and leg lift, flex right heel and simultaneously lift up left foot in a relevé. Press down on floor with arms and hands since this improves balance and lift effect. Repeat both variations twice each for both sides of body using any suitable rhythm.

132. Initial position: First position parallel, bend legs pulling knees up to chest. Hug knees and stretch spinal column out from coccyx as far as possible. Stretch thorax as well, relax neck, do not raise shoulders. Place weight on feet in order to bring calf muscles into play.

132

133. Starting in coccyx slowly roll spinal column back. Be aware of each individual vertebra (stepladder effect). Maintain hug. From vertical position to beginning of roll-back (forehead touches knees), count slowly from 1 to 4, simultaneously exhaling. Movement in this exercise is smooth and flowing.

134. Again start spine and thorax stretch in coccyx and go up the ladder. Hugging knees adds to the lift. Inhale with stretch.

135. Return to initial position with a 1 to 4 count. Make sure that pelvis does not move back during stretch and that legs remain drawn up at a sharp angle with respect to body. Repeat exercise four times. Exhale when rolling back spinal column, inhale when extending.

136. From initial position as in fig. 132 move first left arm, then right out to side. Keep spine and thorax stretched.

137. Making sure not to move pelvis, extend left leg in a diagonally raised position. Keep other leg bent. Stretch thigh, knee, foot. In this position, bounce leg up about 8 times. Do not move thorax. Return left leg to starting position. Bend in suspended position and then set down. Short pause and then other side. Each side twice, any suitable rhythm. Breathe freely.

136   **137**

138. Initial position: Sitting position, legs crossed, right leg in front, right hand holding right heel, both knees straight out, thorax and free hand relaxed.

139. Slowly stretch right leg forward, maintaining hold on heel. Stretch thorax and spine simultaneously with leg movement. Similar to bending a spring.

140. Stretch leg diagonally upward as far as it will go. Center of gravity is middle of pelvis.

140f. Not like this! Keep back straight during leg stretch.

141

141. Move extended leg out to side. Maintain rest of body placement.

142

142. Continue by flexing heel. Maintain grip, breathing will regulate itself.

143

143. Extend foot again bending knee at the same time. This affects all of right thigh. Return to initial position. Short pause and then switch to other side. Repeat twice for both sides with a suitable rhythm. The slower the exercise is carried out, the more thoroughly the body has to work.

144. Body concentration: Stretch body from head to foot and at same time try to spread it out on the floor. Forearms and hands squared off on floor. Forehead touches floor. Be aware of body pressure on floor. Legs are parallel and together. Breathe easily. Focus mind on body and attune body accordingly. Take about 5 to 8 minutes for this.

145. First phase: Back lift: Hands locked behind neck; elbows, forearms raised; lower legs and feet also raised. Thighs, pelvis and thorax remain on floor. Hold tension a moment, then drop back down. Repeat 4–6 times and then pause.

146. Second phase: High back lift: Basically as in fig. 145; move elbows, thorax and legs upwards towards ceiling as if feet and head were trying to meet. Drop back down. Repeat 4–6 times.

147. Third phase: Push lift: Hands on floor, extend arms and bend thorax back following through with head. Lower legs and feet are simultaneously raised towards head. Drop back down. Repeat 4 times.

148. Fourth phase: Hammock lift: Grip feet ankles and pull up thorax, legs to make body look like a hanging hammock. Stretch arms, relax neck, breathe freely. Slowly relax and then again bend up. Repeat 4 times.

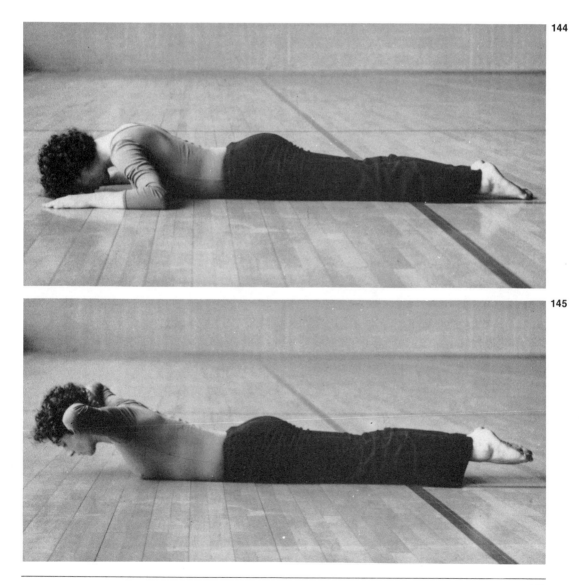

144

145

146

147

148

149f

149f. Do not move pelvis. Keep pelvis pressed to floor during leg lift.

149. Thorax lift with raised arms and elbows. At the same time, right leg (extended) is raised. Pelvis and lower thorax remain on floor. Repeat alternately 4 times on both sides. Rise up quickly, go back down slowly.

149

150f

150f. How not to do it. Pelvis is moved out of place, defeating the purpose of exercise.

150. Second phase: Thorax and leg lift combined with flexed heel. Repeat 4 times on either side. Lift quickly, glide back down.

151. Third phase: Thorax and leg lift with plié. Thighs remain on floor. Feet are extended. Repeat 4 times on each side.

150

151

152. Again in combination: Lift, plié and heel flex.
Repeat 4 times on both sides. Breathing: inhale
on lift, exhale when returning to floor.

153. Hands on floor, elbows slightly bent. Torso held steady. Both legs in first position parallel relevé. From this position, execute a battement extending leg until a line is created running from heel to head. Do not move rest of body, especially pelvis. Repeat 4 times on either side, preferably in 3/4 time. Battement on 1, pause on 2, back down slowly on 3.

154. Concentrate on keeping thorax and pelvis in position, stretch out spinal column. Very good exercise for entire torso region.

155. Execute battement with flexed heel. Basically as in fig. 153. Repeat 4 times on either side. Breathe freely. Head is bent back slightly.

156. Initial position as in fig. 153. Begin by pulling left knee up to chest as in a passé. Leave right leg extended and raised.

156

157. Immediately execute battement (parallel) straight back to the position indicated . . .

157

158. . . . and then turn in a thorax twist. Left foot is put down on ball. Right half of body turns in other direction so that strong twisting effect results. Eyes are focused on floor. From this position, go directly back to initial position. Repeat exercise 4 times on either side, preferably in 3/4 time with extended twist phase.

158

159

159. Initial position: Body weight distributed evenly on both lower legs. Square off thorax. Stretch out spinal column and extend arms downwards to heels. Body center is pelvis center. Slow tempo, preferably with a count of 8.

160

160. Begin vertebral roll-back in coccyx. Pelvis moves down towards floor, hands grip heels. Thorax and head are curved forward.

161

161. Keep hands on heels. Push pelvis and thighs forward from coccyx. Weight evenly distributed on lower legs.

162

163

162. Continue movement until spinal column is
bent back at almost a right angle to pelvis and thighs
(focus mind on vertebral ladder analogy). Keep head
and neck relaxed, maintain grip, stretch pelvis and
thighs to the limit and hold.

163. Then release pelvis, let head hang back loosely, focus eyes on ceiling. Pelvis slowly moves down
to floor. Thorax is vertical.

164

164. When pelvis is almost on floor, thorax lashes forward (lead with chest) . . .

165

165. . . . until thorax is rolled together in front and spinal column is strongly rounded. Keep head relaxed, feel center of movement in pelvis. From here . . .

166. . . . extend spinal column from center, pelvis rises, thorax moves forward, i. e. back to the initial position. Raise back of head, focus eyes vertically on floor. These small details help in carrying out the movements and in positioning the body correctly. Repeat 4 times to a count of 8 before and 8 after release. Let breathing come freely.

166

3

Isolation Exercises

To isolate in this context means to single out or to separate. In this set of exercises, the whole body is divided up into individual zones or fields of movement and gone through phase by phase from top to bottom. Body consciousness, coordination, reflexes and reactions are systematically and intensively trained. The scale of movement and of expression is thus considerably enlarged. By isolating the body into individual movement centers, the principle of multiplication – so important in jazz dance – is realized almost effortlessly. The body seen as an instrument becomes an incarnation of dance principles. There is no doubt that isolation training is considered very important in everyday dance practice.

Centers of Movement

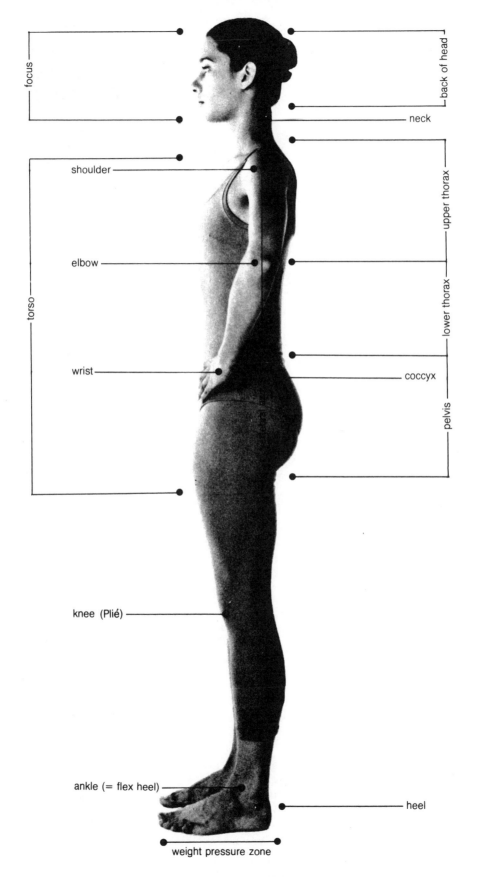

focus

back of head

neck

shoulder

upper thorax

elbow

lower thorax

torso

wrist

coccyx

pelvis

knee (Plié)

ankle (= flex heel)

heel

weight pressure zone

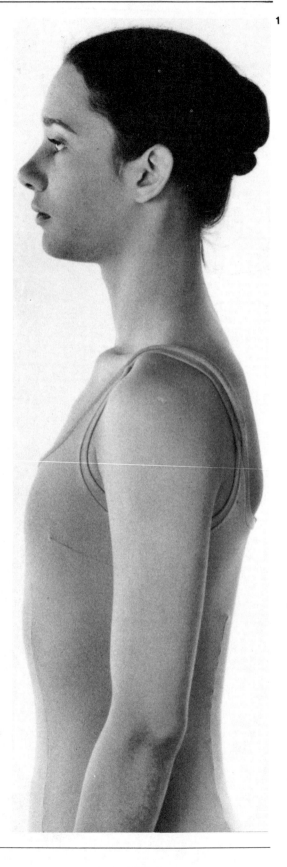

1. Initial position: First position parallel (see note p. 21). Stretch and extend body and spinal column straight up from heels to back of head. Breathe deeply and easily.

2

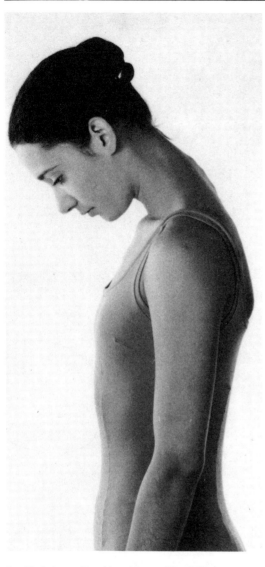

3

3A

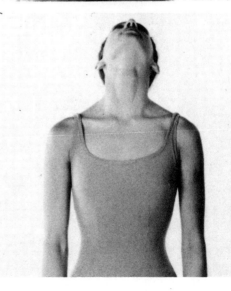

2. First phase: Bend head forward in gliding motion . . .

3. . . . and then back again. Relax forehead and face.

3A. Do not strain neck, keep shoulders relaxed. Repeat 8 times in 2/4 time.

4

4. Second phase: Assume initial position.

5

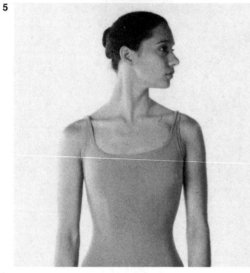

5. Turn head sharply to left . . .

6

6. . . . and then to right. Turn head around axis without changing body position.

7. Third phase: Bend head to right side. Neck is stretched.

8. Now bend to left side. Repeat 8 times on either side with a gliding movement. Any suitable rhythm.

7f. Do not turn head. Keep face looking straight ahead.

7f

7

8

9. Fourth phase: From initial position, thrust head forward (as if stretching to see something more clearly . . .

10. . . . and then in a gliding motion, move head straight back (if you had eyes in the back of your head they would be looking straight ahead). Repeat 8 times in 2/4 time.

9

10

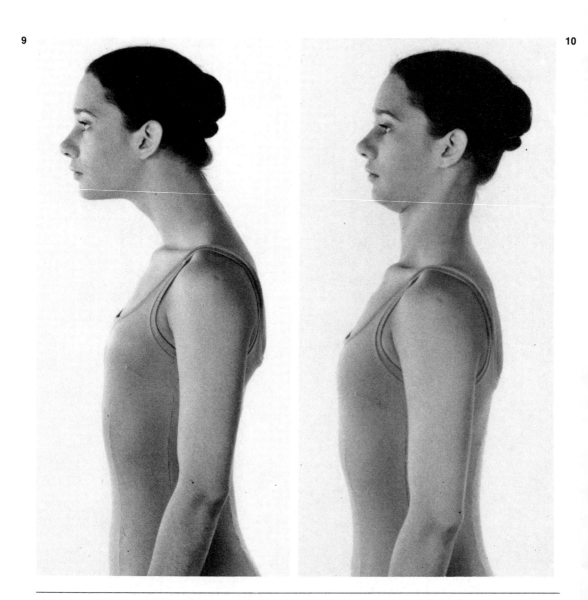

11. Fifth phase: Reassume initial position.

12. Move head to right without bending neck to side. Rather short movement.

13. Now to left. Focus eyes to front. Repeat 4 times on both sides. Execute slowly using any suitable rhythm.

12

13

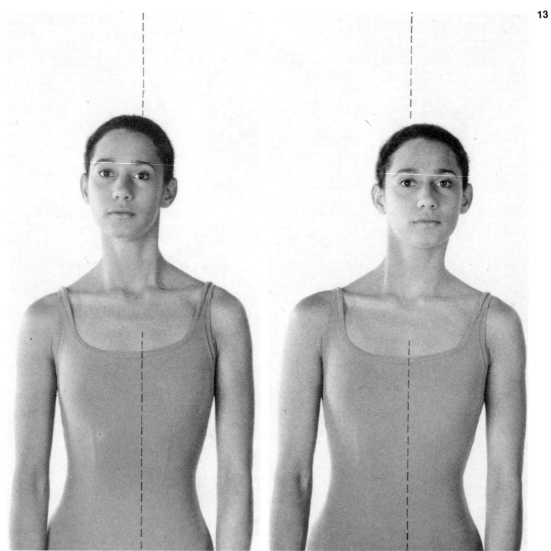

14. Sixth phase: Initial position: Head moves down and forward, neck relaxed.

15. Moving around to right and back . . .

16. . . . then to left . . .

17. . . . and back to front position. From here revolve back around in opposite direction. Repeat 4 times in either direction, preferably in flowing 4/4 time. Head should turn easily and smoothly as if supported by a ball bearing.

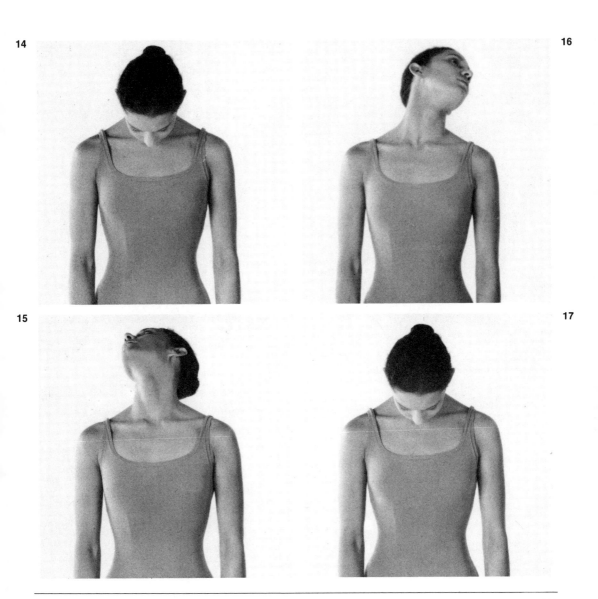

18

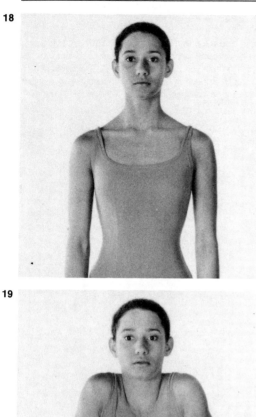

19

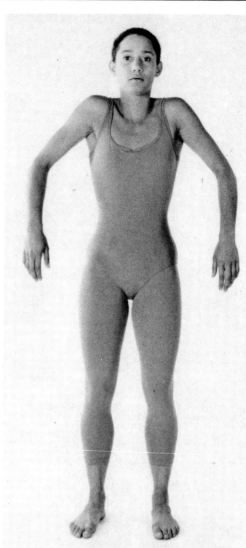

20

18.   Reassume initial position. Placement exactly as in fig. 1.

19.   First phase: Pull both shoulders up. Arms hang completely relaxed from shoulder sockets.

20.   Keep shoulders raised; bend both elbows up.

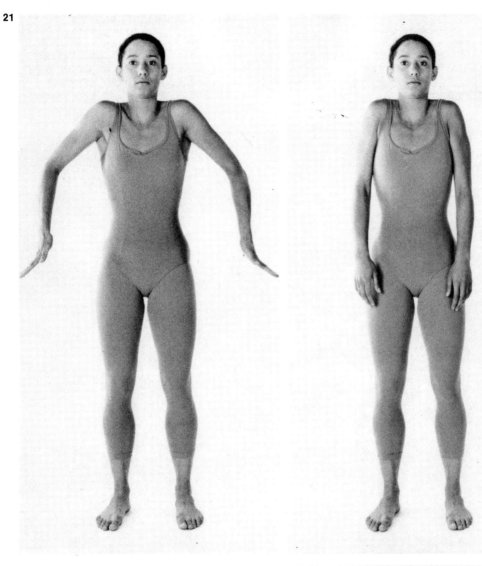

21. Bend both hands outwards. Three active centers are formed: shoulders, elbows, hands. From this position . . .

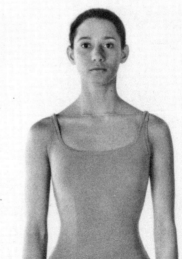

22. . . . relax arms and hands. Shoulders stay in place, i. e. raised.

23. Now relax shoulders, too. Repeat exercise 4 times, a count of 6 being best. Shoulders up on 1, bend elbows up on 2, bend hands out on 3, relax arms on 4, relax shoulders on 5, pause on 6.

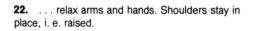

24. Second phase: Shoulders moved separately. Only left shoulder. Pull up and relax.

25. Now right shoulder. Keep alternating. Execute in 2/4 time, flowing motion. Repeat 4 times on either side.

26. Third phase: Shoulder gyrations: Both shoulders move forward and upward in a circular motion . . .

27. . . . and then backward and downward. Repeat 4 times starting with forward motion and 4 times starting with backward motion. Execute in moderate 4/4 time. Important: Generate movement from shoulder joint.

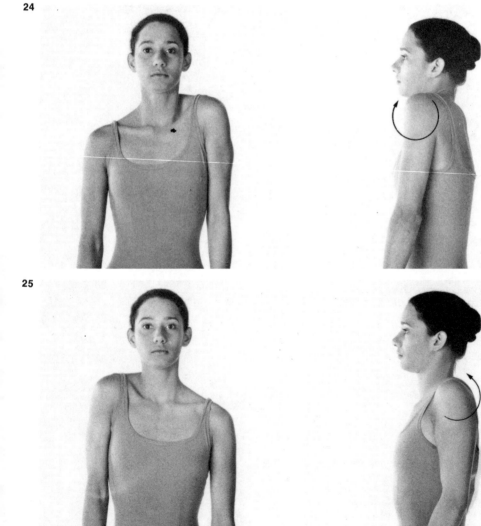

24

26

25

27

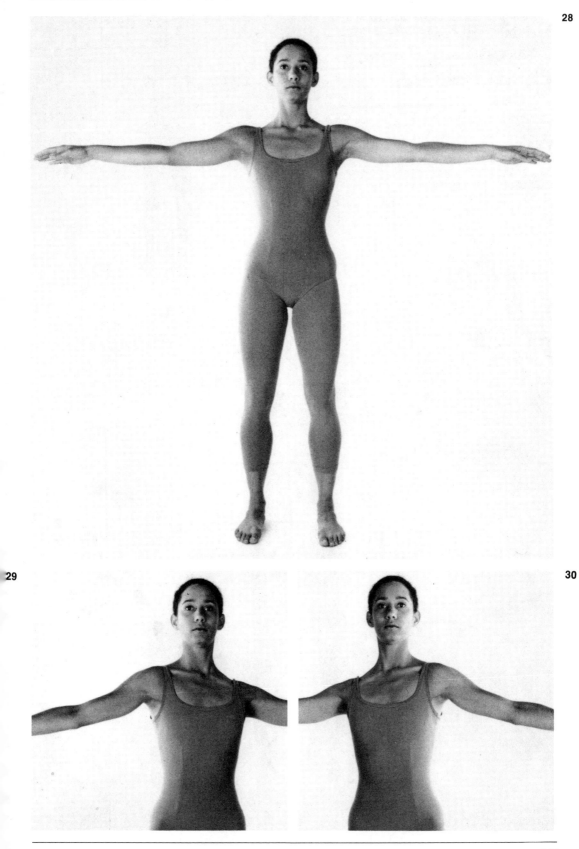

28. From initial position extend arms out to either side. Palms of hands are turned towards floor.

29. Push right shoulder in front (in detail) . . .

30. . . . after to the left (see also 31/32)

31. First phase: Push left shoulder forward simult-aneously pulling right shoulder back towards spinal column.

32. Repeat immediately on other side putting right shoulder forward and pulling left shoulder back. Four repetitions in accentuated 2/4 time.

31

32

33. Second phase: Raise arms up diagonally and from here . . .

34. . . . again push right shoulder forward while left shoulder is pulled back. Head and eyes go with movement and focus is parallel to arm . . .

35. . . . now alternate, left forward, right back. Repeat 4 times in same rhythm. Important: keep arms straight out to side.

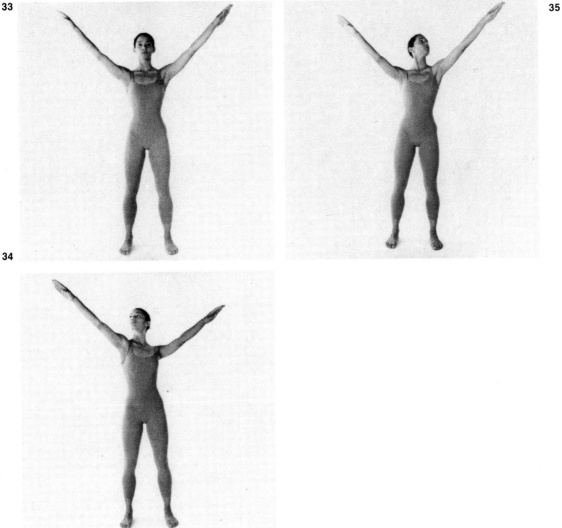

33

35

34

36

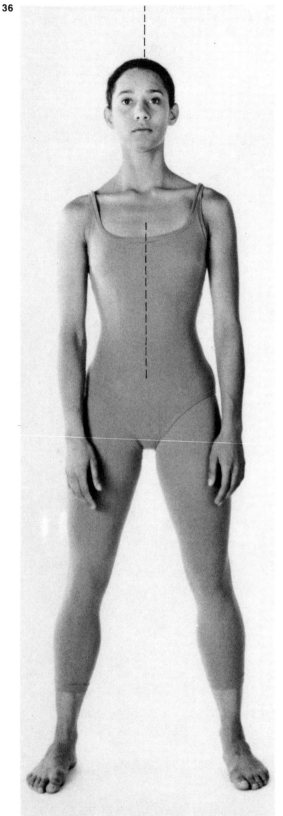

36. Assume initial position. Space legs a little farther apart, slightly turned out. Be aware of centerpoint (pelvis).

37. First phase: Stretch right side of thorax (do not raise shoulder) simultaneously contracting left side. Movement is small and delicate.

38. Alternating, stretch left side of thorax contracting right side. Arms are relaxed. Repeat 4 times a on either side in 3/4 time.

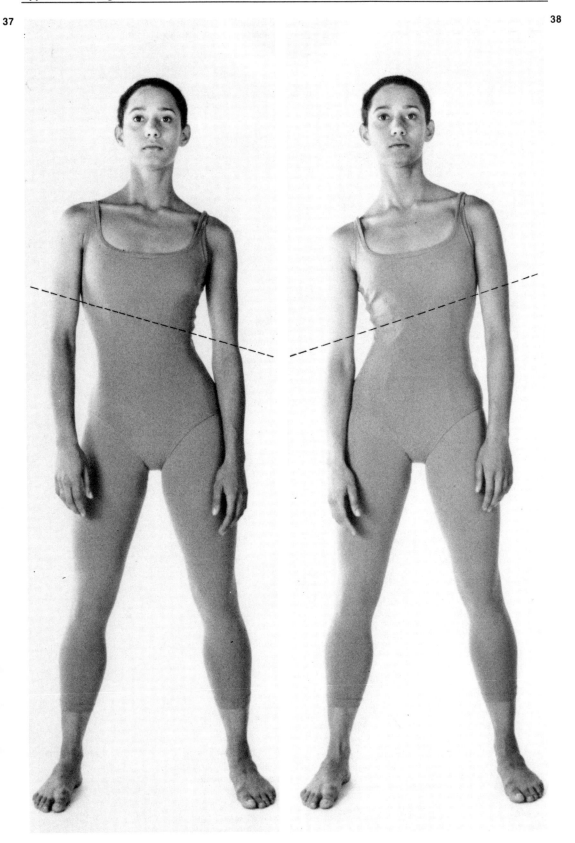

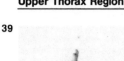

39

39. Second phase: Extend arms up vertically, palms facing in. Do not pull shoulders up.

40. Stretch right side of thorax (like a rubber band) simultaneously contracting directly under juncture of arm and shoulder.

41. Changing sides simultaneously stretch on left and contract on right. Repeat 4 times in 3/4 time. Eyes are focused straight ahead.

42. From initial position assume second position slightly turned out. Lay hands on shoulders and raise upper arms out to either side. Eyes focused straight ahead.

43. First phase: Move thorax to right. Do not bend. Move to side without changing rest of body positioning.

43A. Basically the same exercise. Arms are extended to either side, legs wide in second position slightly turned out. Push thorax to right as far as it will go. Do not raise shoulders and keep pelvis in position.

44. Same to left. Repeat on both sides 8 times in flowing 2/4 time.

44A. Same movement to left. Do not bend thorax. Repeat in both directions 4 times in gliding tempo. Let breathing come freely.

43   43A

44   44A

45. Initial position in second position slighly turned out. Again hands on shoulders and upper arms straight out to side. Twist thorax vigorously to right . . .

45A. . . . around spinal column into a diagonal position. Keep neck relaxed, upper arms out at right angles, eyes focused straight ahead.

45B. Keep thorax twisted and move it such that it describes a figure eight. Pull thorax diagonally forward and to left, then further to left and back, then diagonally forward to right etc.

45   **45A**

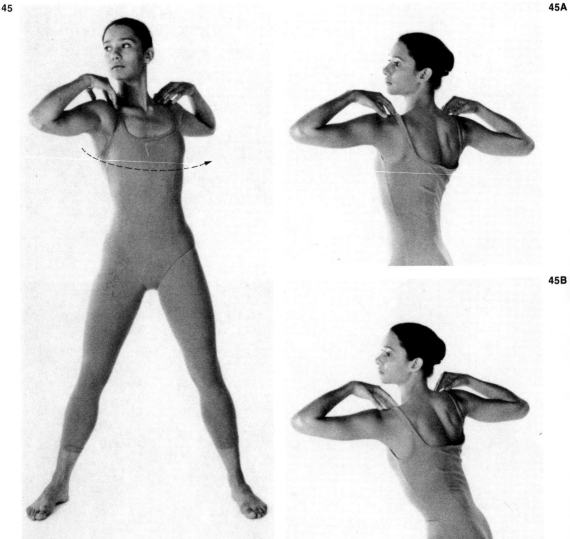

45B

46. Thorax twist visible here. Important: Keep pelvis stiff, do not turn it with thorax.

46A. From forward left semicircle move back to diagonal position.

46B. Thorax twist diagonally to right. Do not raise shoulders. Head follows through. Do 4 figure eights using one 3/4 measure for every semicircle, or four 3/4 measures for one figure eight.

46   **46A**

                                                                          46B

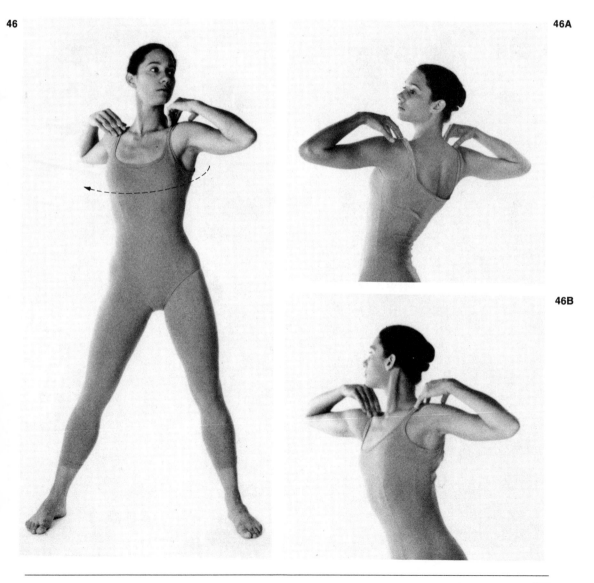

47. Begin in second position slightly turned out. Place hands on hips. Stretch entire body and hold it steady. Keep eyes focused ahead.

48. Not moving pelvis, push thorax ahead slightly (think of ball bearing image). Keep steady. Chest leads movement.

49. From here move thorax directly back. Continue to hold it steady. Elbows remain slightly bent. Keep foundation (pelvis, legs) as firm as concrete.

50. Back again to center as in fig. 47. Move thorax back and forth on top of immobile pelvis. Repeat 6–8 times in a free and gliding rhythm.

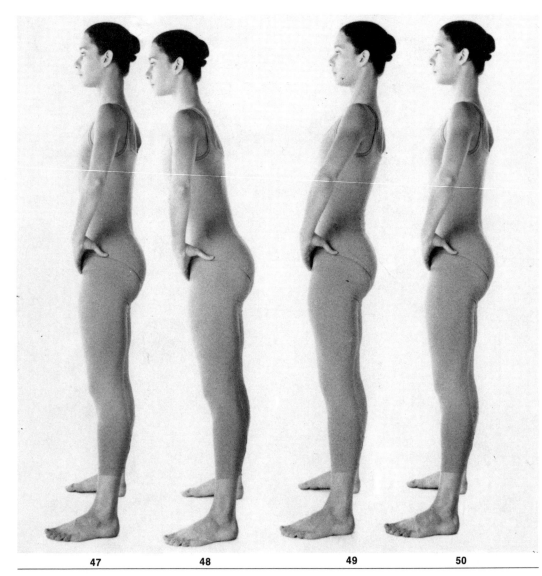

47   48   49   50

51. Again second position. A vertical axis runs through body out into space. Hands on hips.

52. Simultaneously head bends forward and pelvis contracts. Pull pelvis in under thorax.

53. Release pelvis and head at same time. Neck relaxed. Repeat 8 times in gliding motion. This way simultaneous tensions can be experienced better.

54. In the final position re-establish vertical axis. Do not neglect breathing.

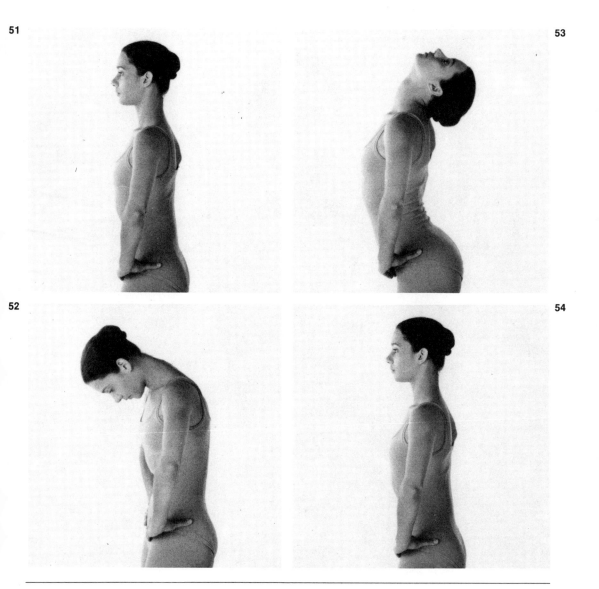

51

53

52

54

55. First phase: Place hands lightly on shoulders and extend upper arms straight out at either side. In initial position push pelvis to right. Focus eyes straight ahead. Important: Maintain center of gravity and distribute weight evenly on both feet.

55f. Do not distribute weight unevenly and cause pelvis to sag.

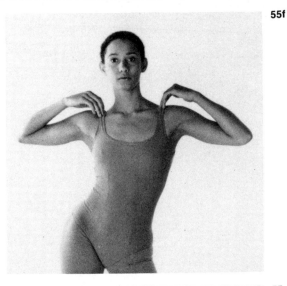

55f

55

56. Push pelvis to left. Lift in pelvis can clearly be seen here. Repeat 4 times on either side moving directly from side to side with gliding motion, free rhythm.

56B. Another variant. Both hands touch inner edge of hip joint. This may make it easier for some people to develop a feel for pelvis isolation. Distribute weight evenly on both feet.

57. Second phase: Pelvis and low thorax region in left. Upper thorax region is isolated with both hands (photo).

57B. Check body centerpoint and vertical axis again.

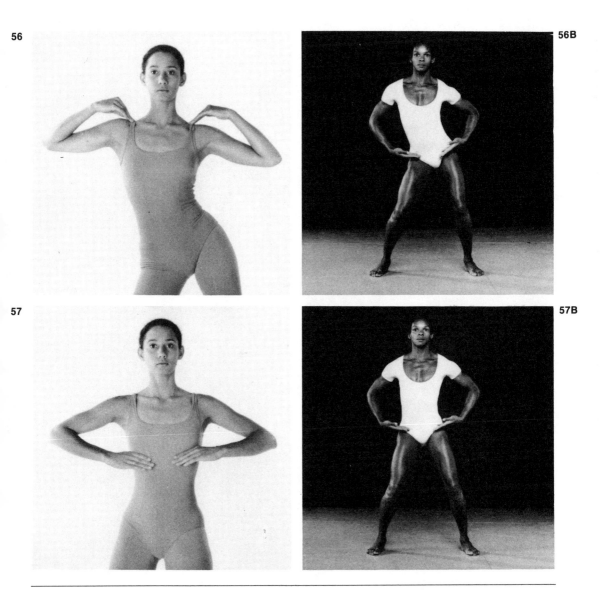

56

56B

57

57B

58

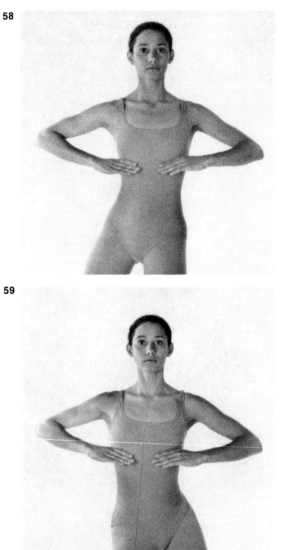

59

58. Move pelvis lift to right. Upper thorax region does not move.

59. Directly back again to left. Maintain body vertical. Repeat 4 times on either side with gliding motion and free rhythm.

60

60. Lift pelvis to left. Left side of thorax just under left arm simultaneously contracts. Repeat 4 times on either side.

61. Third phase: Lift pelvis again to right simultan eously bending head to right. Arms hang relaxed. Important: Keep face to front. Do not turn head. Keep pelvis in position. Contract thorax under right arm.

61

62. First phase: Start in second position slightly turned out and demi plié. Contract pelvis, bend head forward, arms extend straight out in a closed circle, spinal cord is slightly rounded. Important: place weight evenly on both legs and maintain central axis.

62

63. Release pelvis (hollow back) simultaneously pulling elbows straight back. Head bends back, eyes are focused on ceiling, shoulders are pulled together in back. You should have the feeling you are being pulled straight up in the air. Maintain demi plié throughout exercise. Repeat 4 times in a gliding rhythm.

63

64. Second phase: Second position turned out. Arms are opened to sides and bent up slightly, palms up. Distribute weight evenly on both legs.

64A. Bend thorax to right (keep legs and pelvis in position). Simultaneously raise left arm up over head; push right arm down and over to right as illustrated keeping arm close to thorax. Repeat 4 times in slow rhythm.

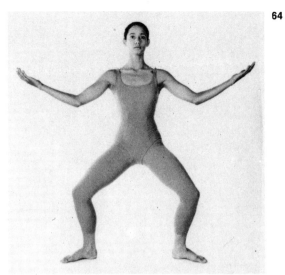

64

64A

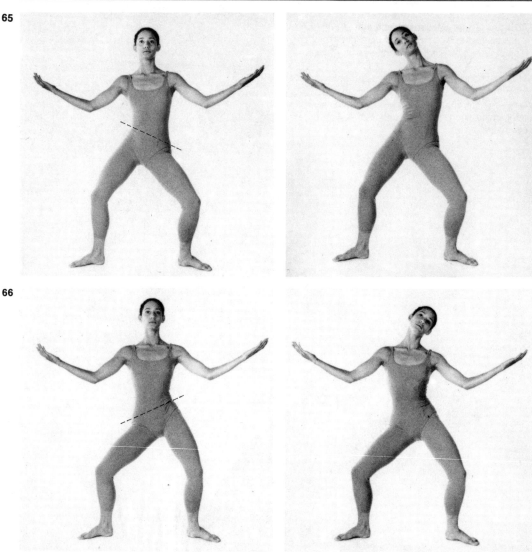

65. Third phase: From second position lift pelvis up to right. Weight remains equally distributed.

66. Then lift to left. After 4 lifts on either side . . .

67. . . . include head in exercise. Contract slightly in upper thorax (right) . . .

68. . . . and then switch sides. Keep arms out, eyes looking straight ahead. Repeat 4 times slowly keeping movements under control.

69

69. Begin in second position turned out. Place backs of hands in small of back. Simultan eously contract pelvis (especially right half), bend right leg raising right foot, shift weight to right. Ball of right foot stays on floor. Left leg remains extended. Keep thorax and head in position. Then release back into second position.

70. Now left side. Contract pelvis strongly. Bring thighs into play.

71. A variation with arms and head. Here we have contraction in pelvis, thigh, knee and foot. Positioning and weight distribution easily recognizable. In this variation, arms are slightly bent, hands and wrists relaxed.

71f. Do not release and let head fall back.

71

70

71f

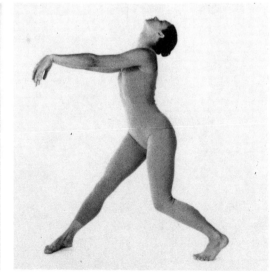

72. First phase: Begin in first position parallel (see exercise 1, fig. 1). Place hands on front of hips. Bend arms slightly and hold straight out to sides.

73. Torso and head (eyes to front) remain straight. Go into demi plié.

74. Add relevé. Keep weight even on balls of both feet.

75. Still in relevé extend legs, establish center axis, be aware of spinal column.

76. From vertical stretch bend torso back (from knee to head) to a diagonal position. Maintain releve. Most important here are thigh, pelvis and abdominal muscles. From here reverse exercise returning to vertical position in relevé, straighten legs, come down on floor powerfully with both heels. Repeat 4 times, preferably with a count of 1 to 8. Important: Keep torso stable feeling its presence in space, especially in vertical position.

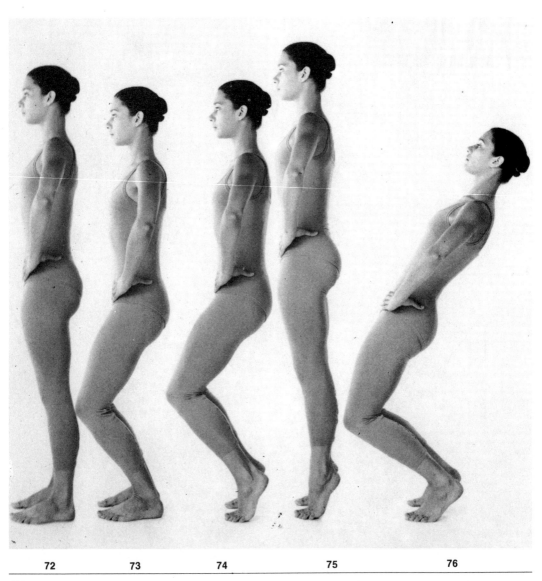

     72   73   74   75   76

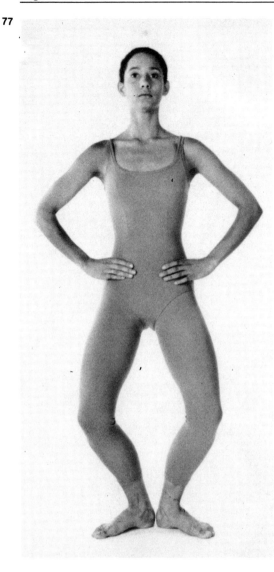

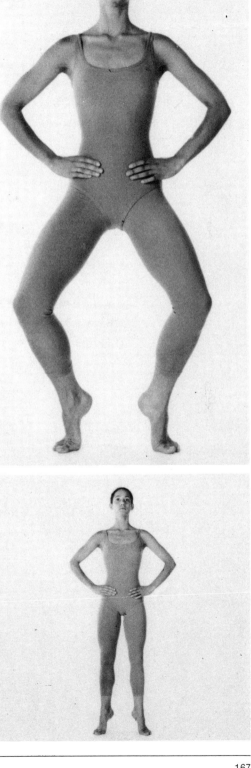

77. Second phase: First position turned out and demi plié. Press heels down on floor. Maintain centerpoint in pelvis region, eyes focused ahead.

78. Rise up in relevé (calf muscles in play). Hands are placed loosely on hips. Neck is relaxed. Breathe freely.

79. Extend legs in relevé. Come back down on heels with legs extended. Repeat 4 times in 2/4 time. Keep torso stable.

80

81

82

80. Third phase: Same exercise again. This time
in second position turned out. Place hands on shoulders such that torso is free. Distribute weight evenly
on both legs.

81. Go into demi plié. Keep pelvis stable (in place).

82. Add relevé. Concentrate on calf and thigh muscles.

83. Rise up on legs in relevé. Be conscious of
lift in whole body. Set heels back down leaving legs
straight. Repeat 4 times in 2/4 time.

83

84

85

86

84. Fourth phase: Second position parallel, arms opened out to side, palms facing forward, fingers spread. Again go into demi plié and add relevé.

85. After straightening legs in relevé bend straightened thorax forward to an angle of 90 degrees. Reach out on either side with arms. Focus eyes on floor. Maintain balance in relevé. Then move thorax back into vertical position coming down on heels with legs straight. Repeat exercise 4 times with gliding motion and a count of 1–8.

86. Fifth phase: Begin in fourth position parallel. Place hands on shoulders. Keep torso stable and stretch out spinal column. Eyes straight ahead. Go into demi plié, add relevé.

86A

86A. Maintain relevé and lean torso (plus right knee and head) back in diagonal position. Left arm is extended forward, right arm out to right side. Hold tension in thigh, pelvis. By no means make a back bend out of this exercise.

87

87. Torso returns to vertical position, relevé is held, hands are placed back on shoulders.

88. Then bend thorax forward from pelvis at a 90 degree angle simultaneously reaching out with arms and focusing on floor. Extend spinal column. Keeping legs straight, slowly come down on heels and return thorax to vertical position. Place hands back on shoulders. Repeat 4 times in 2/4 time with a count of 1–8. This exercise requires strength and tranquility.

88

89. Initial position: Second position slightly turned out. Weight is shifted to left leg. Keep pelvis stable (do not tip to one side). Right leg lightly touches floor on ball of right foot (no weight!). Arms are extended to either side. Eyes are focused straight ahead. Keep body vertical throughout exercise.

89

90f

90

91

92

90. From passé position, swing foot out sideways to extended position.

90f. Do not let pelvis sag. Keep it lifted.

91. From side swing forward. This creates twist tension in support leg and thorax. Keep eyes focused forward. From this position . . .

92. . . . swing leg out to side (keeping support leg straight) and back (free leg parallel). Support leg goes into demi plié. From here swing out to (right) side, forward, to side and back. Repeat 4 times in flowing 4/4 time. Important: free leg is bent, foot extended during swing exercise. Support leg bends only when swinging back and straightens again in swing to side. Keep center axis constant.

4

Position and Space

Everything that has been organically and systematically developed in the three previous sections of this book will be applied in this section.
The body, or body technique, has now reached maturity and a state of self-reliance. At this point a breakthrough into space takes place. The main emphasis here is on conscious training of coordination in movement, intelligence in movement, dynamics and a sense of space.
A feeling for form, kinetics, balance, timing and rhythm is also important. On this basis movement patterns can lead to conscious experience of motion. The body as an instrument becomes a refined body transformed into dance, a pure expression of dance, as it were.

1. First phase: Start in fourth position parallel (opened fairly wide). Stand firmly in demi plié placing weight evenly on both legs. Left foot is bent up (weight on ball of foot). Centerpoint in pelvis, extend thorax, spinal column, eyes directed straight ahead. Arms extended and hands spread in reach-out. Neck relaxed.

1

2

2. Rasie left foot up to right knee (passé), maintain demi plié.

2A. Now a combination: drop – step / kick – relevé. Lift left leg in passé (as in fig. 2) simultaneously letting arms sink relaxed to sides. Thorax is bent forward, support leg in demi plié. From this position . . .

2 A

3. ... extend forward parallel. Maintain demi plié. Important: execute in one continous movement: starting position, passé, kick forward. From extended position back right away to starting position. Repeat 4 times on both sides in flowing 2/4 time.

4. Second phase: Starts out in principle like in fig. 1. Now, however, kick is executed with relevé. Support leg straightened and foot raised. Keep balance. From this position directly back to starting position. Repeat 4 times on either side in flowing 2/4 time.

5. As a further variation (legs are parallel) kick can be carried out in relevé with heel flexed.

3

4A

4

4A. Sharp kick forward (parallel), simultaneously stretching thorax. Hold arms out away from sides, support leg is in demi plié – relevé (weight on ball of foot). Focus eyes straight ahead, maintain balance. From here directly back to starting position. Repeat 4 times on either side, free rhythm, but accentuated. Primary movement is drop-step and kick.

5

6. From fourth position parallel (see fig. 1) move left leg from behind far forward. Simultaneously: Right leg in demi plié, contract pelvis, bend thorax forward, extend head straight out (focus eyes on floor), arms are extended along with head. Important: be consciously aware of centers of movement. From this position return to initial position. Repeat 4 times on either side in free rhythm. Step forward is snappy. Extend pause somewhat. Let breathing come by itself.

6

6A. This is a variation with right leg forward and
left leg behind. Arms slightly different, a little softer,
rounded inwards. Pelvis is contracted, thorax bent
forward, weight distributed evenly on both feet.

6A

7A. Another combination: kick with thorax back. Basically same pattern except that thorax and arms are rounded forward. From here . . .

8A. . . . again passé. Support leg remains in demi plié. Arms are extended.

7. Second phase: Fourth position – basically as in fig. 1. Legs turned out, left heel raised slightly placing weight only on ball of foot. Extend arms and hands diagonally downward. Stretch thorax. Neck relaxed.

8. Pull up right leg (foot extended) in passé, simultaneously straightening support leg. Press heel to floor.

7A   **7**

8A   **8**

9. Extend right leg back in arabesque. Important: When free leg goes into arabesque support leg goes into demi plié and extended thorax is bent forward. Arms are extended out to sides. Execution is in one flowing movement from initial position. Spinal column and thorax remain straight. Let movement flow in space. Repeat 4 times on either side in free rhythm.

9A. Kick back. Simultaneously bend thorax back, focus eyes upward, move arms back diagonally, palms face down. Maintain demi plié in support leg. Open pelvis slightly to side. Countermove thorax. From here go directly back to initial position. Repeat 4 times in free rhythm.

9

9A

10

10. Third phase: Side kick. Start in fourth position slightly turned out and all the way down. Weight is placed evenly on both legs. Left heel is slightly lifted and weight on ball of foot. Fingertips on floor. Eyes straight ahead. Centerpoint in pelvis. From here . . .

10A. Another variation: lower left leg and knee flat on floor with weight on it. In one continuous motion through passé . . .

10A

11. ... go through passé to side kick. Stretch support leg as much as possible. Do not let pelvis move to right.

11

11A. ... to side kick (leg extended straight out).
Support leg goes into relevé (sequence plié, relevé).
Important: straightly held thorax is bent forward at
same time. Arms and hands are extended out on
either side (helpful!). Eyes are focused straight ahead.
Repeat 4 times on either side with free rhythm.

11A

12   **12A**

12B

12. Kick into raised extended position. Lift thorax. From extended position straight back to floor position. Here, too, it is important that kick be executed in one continuous movement. Requires strength, especially in thigh area. Repeat 4 times on either side; 3/4 time is recommended.

12A. Side kick is executed from floor position with heel flexed. Support leg in releve. Watch thorax and pelvis positions.

12B. Variation: Free leg more or less parallel. Support leg goes into relevé. Kick leg up and out to side as far as possible. Bend thorax forward at same time (nearly 90 degrees). Stretch out spinal column. Extend arms far out to side and pull up slightly. From here . . .

12C. Extend free leg straight back and bend up. Support leg is in demi plié. Arms and head go in direction of movement. Maintain twist tension in thorax. From here slowly lower free leg and return to floor position. Execute only after heaving mastered basic movements.

12C

13. Initial position: Cross right leg with left and place ball of foot on floor. Relax arms and stretch torso. Focus eyes ahead.

14. Going through passé kick free leg straight out, at same time raising arms and hands diagonally up and outward. Neck is relaxed. Do not raise shoulders.

15. Return to initial position (transitional phase), setting ball of foot down firmly . . .

14

13

15

16. ... and move right leg far back, falling to floor. Come down on ball of foot. Simultaneously flex left heel. Thorax is in angular tension. Stretch out spinal column. Fingertips are on floor. From this position, directly execute a forward kick so that right crosses left (transitional phase) and sides are switched automatically. Repeat 4 times in free rhythm. Important: Always concentrate on making kick and fall one fluid movement and that transitions and changes of sides are smooth.

16

17. First form: From first position parallel execute glide step to side, support leg goes into demi plié. Elbows are extended out, forearms closed in front of chest, hands hang down relaxed. Eyes are focused straight ahead. Move right leg forward and across (in demi plié) so that left leg goes into sideways glide. Practice this step in a soft blues rhythm back and forth across the room.

17

18. Second form: Again glide step but arms varied. Simultaneously with glide step raised opposite arm, hand remains relaxed. When right leg moves forward and across arm moves back, when leg moves back arms close again in front of chest.

18

19. Start in floor position. Palms face forward. Thorax is stretched upward. Then . . .

19

20. ... place right leg back, slightly diagonally. Extend arms out from front position, relax hands, flex left heel. Extend left leg, right leg in demi plié and ...

20

21. ... bend right leg sharply in passé (parallel). Pull over to support leg (placing entire weight on foot). Follow through with arms, hands, head (left of support leg) and quickly set down right leg.

22. Move left leg out to side and cross around to back (as in a ronde de jambe) with foot just above floor (croissé). Left leg is now support leg (in demi plié), open arms and hands wide into space. Then slowly go back to initial (floor) position and change sides. Important: Carry movement into space and concentrate on centers of movement. Execute in a fluid blues rhythm and a count of 8.

21

22

23. From open fourth position moving through passé to relevé kick far forward in diagonal line. Open arms and body into space. Eyes are focused diagonally upward.

23A. Kick with support leg in demi plié, left arm simultaneously raised back, eyes focused diagonally upward.

23

23A

24. From simple kick (support leg in demi plié) raise knee up sharply (passé), support leg simultaneously goes into relevé and arms are opened back wide in diagonal line. Head is leaned back, eyes are focused upward.

23B. Raise right knee (in passé) to chest simultaneously turning thorax (countermovement) towards free leg, support leg is raised up in relevé and arms opened out. Eyes are focused diagonally upward.

24

23B

24A. Extend free leg straight out and lay thorax back, keeping support leg in relevé. Come down far forward with right leg and then repeat.

23C. Then extend free leg, arms follow through (palms down), support leg in relevé, hold thorax twist. From here cross right leg over in front of left setting it down softly in demi plié. Transition for next step.

24A

23C

25. Another variant of forward kick (parallel), pull
passé in close to support leg, extend arms and head
up into space.

26. From fourth position turned out raised side kick, going up in relevé on support leg. Raise opposite arm, right arm follows raised leg, lift thorax, focus eyes diagonally upward.

26

27. Movement executed in wide arch from right to left (support leg remains in relevé). Consciously turn out into space.

28. At cross-over point just before setting foot down bend right knee sharply (passé) causing a slight hesitation in movement (movement-lift). Thorax bends right in slight curve towards free leg (balance is facilitated).

29. Change from left to right at cross-over point.

30. In final phase (just before fall) move left leg forward in fall step. At same time complete arch overhead with left arm so that both arms meet below. Repeat step 4–6 times on either side.

27

29

28

30

31A. Consciously go through movement centers such as pelvis, thorax, shoulders, head and knees, especially in release.

31. Fall to floor in turning twist. Begin in second position parallel demi plié. Strong release in pelvis, head back, eyes looking up, arms pulled back horizontally. Keep thorax, body vertical.

31A   **31**

32A. Then contract. Extend arms forward in closed circle. Bend head forward. From here . . .

32A

33A. . . . fall down on left hand, heels rise up. Important: Be absolutely certain to maintain contraction. Thorax remains straight. Eyes are directed upward. From here . . .

33A

34A. . . . it is easy to move extended arm down to left, torso and knee follow through to left; maintain tension in pelvis.

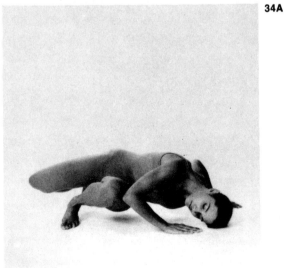

34A

32

32. Thorax and arms are strongly involved here. Initial movement is here, too, pelvis contraction.

33

33. Variation with slight alteration. Arm, hand and head are turned sightly. Heels are pulled up a little higher. Pelvis and thighs are very tense.

34

34. Turning twist again. Torso is held just off of floor. From here either release or other ensuing combinations.

35. Combination: step-twist-fall. Begin in second position parallel. Pull right knee up sharply in open passé simultaneously bending opposite arm (left) up (and extending right arm up in a line with support leg) so that elbow touches knee. Thorax moves counter to lifted leg.

35

36. Then extend free leg far out into space. Thorax is laid back, arms opened up into space (palms out), head back, support leg is kept straight when free leg is fully extended.

36

37. Fall on right leg supporting torso with arms and twisting to left. Body is suspended just above floor.

38. Legs jump up and cross over (right forward, left behind). Arms give strong support.

39. Slowly extend the rear leg (left), shifting weight to torso onto left arm . . .

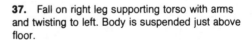

40. ...until leg (or for that matter whole body) is freely suspended. Right arm and hand absorb tension from left leg. Eyes are focused out over right arm, left foot is raised. Keep thorax and pelvis contracted. Then release. Repeat pattern about 4 times for either side.

41. Roll fall: Sit relaxed with right leg crossed over left. Hands are relaxed on floor.

41

42. Roll back on spinal column. Leave legs bent. Press hands and arms on floor for support.

42

43. Roll spinal column back until right leg comes down in big step forward. Arms and hands reach out, thorax is extended. Then . . .

43

44

44. ... extend body far out into diagonal space in relevé. Execute pattern in one continuous flowing movement.

45. Hesitate slightly and then fall precipitately onto hands. Keep arabesque and torso perfectly straight, only bending sharply in pelvis. Remain in relevé, head nearly touches floor.

45A. Good illustration of tension throughout body.

45   **45A**

46

46. Now suspend thorax above floor maintaining arabesque.

47. Slowly bend lower leg over . . .

48. . . . and place foot down so that a twist is created. Counter with left side, right side remains extended. Then release. Repeat 4 times on each side with a double count of 1–8.

47

48

49. Executed basically like a kick (both legs are slightly turned out). Arms are extended forward (palms up). With short approach (no passé) kick free leg forward in direction of movement and leap will come about automatically. Eyes are focused freely in space. Thorax is stretched.

50. Same leap again with sligth modification. When leaving floor as free leg snaps straight forward hesitate a split-second in bent position thus causing a tiny time-delay which enlivens leap.

49
50

51. Bend both legs outward in space; open arms
and hands wide to sides. Leap can be executed
from a standing position or with a running approach

52. Moderated split leap, leg bent back in attitude, front leg extended, arms simultaneously extended (palms down), thorax extended, neck relaxed.

52A. Split leap with flexed heel.

53. Open passé leap to side (feet extended), body stretched up in spece, arms extended to sides, eyes focused straight ahead in space.

54. Forward kick leap (diagonal). Hurtle extended free leg forward such that launching leg is free and can be bent back. Arms are stretched forward, palms up. Thorax is bent slightly in direction of leap. Come down on left foot. Can be executed from standing position, with running approach or in combination with other step patterns, depending on the movement patterns you want to produce.

The Music and the Dance Called Jazz

Jazz feeling is rooted in the physical and psychological feeling for life peculiar to the black African.

Africa: Dance and music are a ritual in community life. The physical ability of the individual and the spirit of the community determine their existence. Every individual is open with respect to the community, and expresses his feelings in it by means of body language. Dancing to the throb of the drums (community life rhythms), the excitement of collective incentive mounts in him to the point of self-surrender (ecstasy) in the bosom of the community.

America: Uprooted, torn out of the context of his community and degraded to cattle, the black African transplanted to the America of the white European. As a toiling slave made submissive by brute force, he was left with only his body, his voice and remembered rhythms to dance and sing away the pain of the present.

As a result of the slave's hopeless situation which was not basically changed by the abolishment of slavery a process of assimilation set in.

Forms of white society and culture were adopted or imposed, as is white religion. They were not, however, assimilated directly but rather modified and given African character. Thus, at the end of the 19th century, we find in the black ghettoes of northern cities European forms with black African feeling. In the churches chorales have become spirituals which have the same physical and ritual meaning as the songs and dances in Africa. In everyday life it is the blues that are the medium for the expression of feelings and here, too, harmonic features are to be found that also occur in European music. Still, blues feeling is the blackest element in jazz. White instruments, too, were adopted: trumpet, trombone, clarinet, saxophone, piano, guitar, bass, tuba and even the drums were not of African, but rather European origin.

As of about the beginning of the 20th century black music began to be known as jazz. Since then an enormous development has taken place. Critics speak of 9 to 10 styles that have a risen, each following its own set of musical laws. But what is behind this development? One reason is certainly the rapid development of American industrial society. The essential reason, though, can be found in an off-the-cuff statement made by an early white jazz musician, Paul Mares.

He described the situation in 1922 this way:

"Really, we had an excellent band. We did our best to play Negro music like we had heard it at home (New Orleans). We did our best but, of course, we couldn't quite copy the Negro style."[1]

This, in itself, is not a problem. Since jazz is improvised music and cannot be preserved in written form the only solution here is to resort to recording methods, records and tapes. This, however, is an economic question. In the recording companies, and there were only white recording companies, at that time, white imitators were preferred to black "creators" in production and advertising, thus creating false celebrities in a style of music alienated from its origins. Blacks saw themselves as robbed of their only possession and ridiculed. Thus, they had to create their music anew. Whites, of course, copied it immediately and this set the process of jazz development in motion. Archie Shepp, an exponent of politically conscious free jazz puts it this way: "New jazz is old jazz. There is really nothing new in it except for a message that hadn't been able to be formulated before today . . . For a long time a character was imposed on black Americans that was not their own."[2]

Black dance suffered the same fate as black music. Relegated to the level of clownery, its natural "show-ability" (revealing, disclosing, manifesting oneself) was exploited in minstrel shows and then adulterated by whites made up to look like blacks, totally corrupting its true message. In the 20's black dance was popularized by white imitations such as the Jitterbug, Charleston and similar dances. In the 30's white imitators such as Fred Astaire and Gene Kelly were made famous by the film industry. Even today jazz dance is still associated with the atmosphere of indecency and vice typical of night clubs.

Jazz both as music and as dance is an expression of a specific feeling for or attitude towards life.

This physical and psychological attitude is certainly not to be found in the files of an archive. Anyone who thinks so has nothing to offer but empty form or technique. As a Central European and having grown up in a tradition that praises the spirit and damns the flesh (what is considered the best European dance is, characteristically, called classic academic dance), it is rather difficult to have this feeling for life. But it is not impossible. It was present at one time in our history and it has merely been covered up. In order to uncover it again it is necessary to create an awareness of the circumstances and reasons for this atrophy. Escape into exotic forms of motion is not a solution. Nor is a return to the origins. This would only mean getting lost in the mists of romanticism. We live in the here and now and this means we have to cope with the situations in today's society and our social surroundings. To overcome the problem of atrophy on the basis of today's society we must involve the individual creatively in the process. Individual improvisation and communication in group improvisation offer ample opportunity for this. This is what we find to be the characteristic feature of the musical and kinetic language called jazz.

The following are a few technical explanations in music that make the described feeling more palpable:

Beat is the basic rhythm of music. It is the regular accented pulsation that makes the rhythm physically felt. It is not a mathematical unit of time like the measure in European music although, for lack of a system of jazz notation, it is described in terms of European music as having 4/4, 3/4 or similar times. For that reason jazz music that appears as a written score can only be an approximation and never an exact registration of the music.

Notes that are not sounded on the beat always lead to the next beat and never away from the previous one. If they are strongly accented they represent a counterweight with respect to the beat and are called off beats.

The simultaneity of beats and off beats creates a multilayered rhythmic dimension that can be attained on the physical plane through isolation technique. Off beats can be so strong that they anticipate the following beat thereby creating the feeling of acceleration without changing the tempo. Between every beat there is a rest phase. This is also the case when several such accelerating accents appear in succession.

The matter can be made clear in notation by identifying the beats and accents with different letters. Let the beat be A, the off beat B and the off beat with the strength of an accelerating accent X.

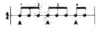

If you try to clap this rhythm while simultaneously tapping out beat A with your foot you will immediately notice a multilayered rhythmic effect, especially when you accentuate B and X more strongly then A. You might be inclined to think that the X's are syncopes, but this is not the case. There are no syncopes in jazz. They are a part of mathematically calculated European music. You must take into consideration that this notation is only an approximation. B and X are not quite halfway between A's. They are closer to the following beat than to the previous one. We can give a better impression of what we mean by writing the rhythm down in triplets.

This "triplet feeling" can be created by taking the first in fast triple beat as A and the third as B or X. The second is either left out or attached to the first.

These rhythmic shifts create the suspended tension known as swing. Duke Ellington called one of his compositions: "It's nothing if it doesn't swing."

In more modern jazz the tempo has, in part, been done away with and the beat is no longer made evident so much by playing it as by playing around it. From swing we have evolved to glide and, consequently, today, no one talks about swinging, but rather about gliding.

The blacks in the Latin American countries created rhythms with accelerating accents that look like different quaver groupings in European notation in which the accent is on the first eight note. Here is one example from many possible ones:

Here, too, the accents between the (European) beats cannot be considered syncopes.

This accentuation and counter-accentuation as well as the distribution of note values is called phrasing. What is meant is that in jazz it is not just a matter of which note to play but much more than that, how you approach playing the note.

Not just the objective is important, but also the way, the motion towards it.

Otto Jansen

Quotes:
1. Shapiro / Henthoff: Jazz erzählt DTV Nr. 69, August 62, p. 70.
2. Interview by Jean-Louis Noames, Jazz Magazine Nr. 125, Paris, December 1965, "Shepp le rébelle", p. 80.

Record suggestions for exercise

Wayne Shorter: Adams Apple Blue Note BLP ST 84232. Rhythms: 3,4 slow, Latin 3/3/2 and more complicated.

John Coltrane: Selflessness Impulse Imp AS 9161. Rhythms: 3 fast, 4 in part free (glide).

Art Blakey and.the Jazz Messengers: Moanin' Blue Note SL ST 84003. Rhythm: moderate and fast 4 with triplet feeling.

Art Blakey: Orgy in Rhythm 8 drummers. Blue Note BL ST 81555. All rhythms.

Art Blakey Quintet: A Night at Birdland Blue Note BL ST 81522. Rhythms: 4, in all tempos – triplet feeling – double time.

Blues and Jazz 25 Years Atlantic Sampler: Atlantic ATL 20052. Rhythms: 4, in all tempos, take five 5.

Dollar Brand African Piano: JAPO Records 60002 Stereo. Rhythms: 5, Ostinato figure.

Suggestions for choreographies

Charlie Mingus: The Black Saint and the Sinner Lady Impulse AS 35.

Circle Paris – Concert: ECM 1018/19 ST.

Gil Evans: Svengall Atlantik ALT 40528.

Besides these records by Thelonius Monk, Charlie Mingus, Miles Davis, John Coltrane, Ornette Coleman, Archie Shepp and others.

I especially recommend working to live music since then a situation arises in which dancers and musicians work on an equal footing. In this way the traditional situation can be overcome, in which musicians produce their music but are excluded from the rest of what takes place and in which dancers are confronted with a finished musical product that they have no way of influencing.

Otto Jansen, born in 1944, has played saxophone since 1960 and has been involved in dance since 1973. At present he is working as a musician and dancer.

Important Literature on the Subject

Raoul Gelabert: "Anatomy for the Dancer", Danad Publishing Co., New York, NY 10019 USA.

Gus Giordano: "Anthology of American Jazz", Orion Publishing House, Evanston, Illinois, USA.

Helmut Günther / Manfred Grimme "Jazz Dance – Theorie und Praxis", Tanzarchiv-Verlag, Cologne.

Helmut Günther: "Grundphänomene und Grundbegriffe des afrikanischen und afroamerikanischen Tanzes", universal edition, Graz, Austria.

Josef Haug / Fred Traguth: "Choreographie heute", Musik und Bildung 12, December 1971, Verlag B. Schott's Söhne, Mainz.

Horst Koegler: "Friedrichs Ballet-Lexikon von A–Z", Friedrich Verlag, Velber bei Hannover, Translated and re-edited as: "The Concise Oxford Dictionary of Ballet", Oxford University Press, London, New York.

Fred Traguth / Dieter Zimmerle: "Jazz Dance", Jazz Podium Nr. 5, May 1970, Verlag Jazz Podium, Stuttgart.